A PECULIAR
OLD

THE IOWA STATE UNIVERSITY PRESS / AMES / 1975

PEOPLE: IOWA'S ORDER AMISH

WITHDRAWN

ELMER SCHWIEDER AND DOROTHY SCHWIEDER

T O   O U R   C H I L D R E N
D I A N E   a n d   D A V I D

ELMER W. SCHWIEDER holds the B.A. degree from Dakota Wesleyan University, the M.S.W. degree from the University of Denver, and the Ph.D. degree from Iowa State University. He is presently associate professor in the Department of Family Environment at Iowa State University. Twice elected Professor of the Year, Dr. Schwieder's research interests are in the area of family, both past and present.

DOROTHY A. SCHWIEDER holds the B.A. degree from Dakota Wesleyan University and the M.S. degree from Iowa State University. She is presently an instructor in the History Department at Iowa State University. Mrs. Schwieder edited the book, *Patterns and Perspectives in Iowa History,* and has published numerous articles on Iowa history. She is a member of the State Historical Board of Iowa.

PHOTOS: **Page i**—ON THE WAY. Photo by Joan Liffring Zug
Title page—THE HELPFUL "FROLIC." Courtesy of the **Des Moines Register and Tribune**

© 1975 The Iowa State University Press
Ames, Iowa, 50010. All rights reserved

Composed and printed by The Iowa State University Press

First edition, 1975
Second printing, 1976
Third printing, 1977

Library of Congress Cataloging in Publication Data

Schwieder, Elmer, 1925-
   A peculiar people.

   Bibliography: p.
   Includes index.
   1. Amish in Iowa. 2. Iowa—History. I. Schwieder, Dorothy, 1933-   joint author.
II. Title.
BX8129.A6S38   977.7   75-23420
ISBN 0-8138-0105-2

CONTENTS

MOVING DAY.

Courtesy of the Des Moines Register and Tribune

The history of the Amish has been a part of the story of Iowa since the early 1840s. The first Amish families moved into Lee County even before the days of Iowa's statehood. Through the years they have expanded in number and settlements and have suffered several schisms, but they have always retained the distinctive qualities that long ago earned for them the name, the "Plain People." With this long-standing settlement in Iowa, it is surprising that so little has been written about the Amish who live in this state. Fortunately, many scholarly studies have been published on Amish populations in Pennsylvania, Ohio, and Indiana; but while some of these findings can be generalized to the entire national Amish population, others cannot. Perhaps even more important, concentration on these eastern areas excludes regional variations as well as the recognition of important mobility trends that are more obvious in the Midwest.

Following a long-time interest in South Dakota's Hutterites, we began to search for written materials on Iowa's Plain People. We were

P R E F A C E

amazed to discover that little was available; if we desired to pursue the topic, there appeared to be only one alternative — to collect the data ourselves. In April 1970 we made our first trip to Kalona to visit the Old Order Amish community there. In the years that followed we returned to Kalona many times as well as traveling on numerous occasions to the settlements in Buchanan County and Milton; later we also visited the Beachy Amish in Leon. In each community we were privileged to meet Amish and non-Amish people who gave generously of their time and energy to assist us with our research.

Because of the nature of our study and the predominance of Old Order among the state's Amish population, we have focused the book primarily on the Old Order group. However, to provide comparisons between the various groups of Plain People who reside in Iowa and other parts of the Middle West, we have included a chapter on the Beachy Amish and minimal comments on other Mennonite groups.

The ''newness'' of the Milton community will be of special interest to students of the American utopian movement. Rarely in historical study is it possible to observe the beginning of such a settlement. We were indeed fortunate to start our study during the initial years of the Milton group. Since 1970 we have followed its development, meeting many of the people moving into the area from surrounding states, and believe that it provides a special dimension to this study.

Our project was a very special one from the beginning. We were continually impressed by the faith and inner peace of the Amish people as well as their ability to insulate themselves against the outside world. As we visited more families and observed such Amish institutions as their parochial schools, our initial impressions developed into a deep, abiding sense of appreciation and profound respect for these people. We feel tremendously fortunate today to count as our friends many Old Order Amish families. We also rediscovered during our many trips around the state that Iowans are friendly, generous people. In every community the townspeople responded willingly with their time to talk with us about their Amish neighbors, particularly in the community of Milton. We came away from these areas with an increased appreciation for the people of Iowa, both Amish and non-Amish.

As the bibliography indicates, we have many people to thank for their time, interest, and enthusiasm in our project. It is not possible to single out everyone, but several individuals must be mentioned. James Frier, Washington County extension director, arranged for our first contacts with Kalona townspeople. We will always be grateful to the late Marie Jackson of Kalona who, deciding that our project sounded worthy, arranged for many of our initial visits with Amish families. Marie was a lifelong resident of Kalona, known and respected by Amish and non-Amish alike, and her approval of our work was invaluable. In Oelwein Mrs. Mary Lacock assisted us in meeting many people in the community who in turn were helpful in making contacts with Amish families. In the Milton area Maxine and Maynard Manske were particularly helpful in assisting with our Amish contacts and revealing many insights into the Old Order Amish life style. Verle and Peggy Arnold of Bloomfield also provided pertinent information. Marlan Logan, a former resident of Kalona, was helpful as a source on the general background of the Kalona community as well as in gathering information on the Beachy Amish settlements in Iowa.

We also wish to thank Mrs. Edith Munro, consultant in elementary education for the State Department of Public Instruction, for discussing the Amish school situation with us and checking the two chapters on Amish education for accuracy. Most helpful in the early stages of our research was an initiatory research grant from the Iowa State University Research Foundation which underwrote the cost of many trips to Kalona and Buchanan County. We are indebted to the Graduate Dean at Iowa State University for providing funds for the typing of the manuscript and also to the History Department for additional typing assistance.

It is especially difficult to select Amish individuals for special thanks because all the families we visited were most hospitable and helpful. Truman Miller and Chris Kauffman, both Old Order Amish bishops, helped us understand the role and selection of religious leaders; Mr. and Mrs. Eddie Miller told us about their farming operations and family life; Mr. and Mrs. Mahlon Mullet were part of the first group to settle in Milton and provided us with insights into the way a new community is established. Two families with whom we had sustained contact and count as our "special friends" are Mr. and Mrs. Tobias J. Miller of Kalona and Mr. and Mrs. Mervin Hershberger of Milton. Perhaps for this reason our view of the Old Order is personified by these individuals. We also wish to thank Tobias Miller and Bishop and Mrs. Glen L. Bender, also of Kalona, for their careful reading of the manuscript and for taking the time to make considerable comment on the text. We feel that their contributions add immeasurably to the integrity and accuracy of the book. The list would be far too long if we named each one, but we wish to thank all the Amish people that we met for their hospitality and assistance, because without their cooperation — and never was this statement more appropriate — this book could not have been written.

"But ye are a chosen generation, a royal priesthood, an holy nation, a peculiar people; that ye should shew forth the praises of him who hath called you out of darkness into his marvellous light."

I Peter 2:9

". . . our Saviour Jesus Christ; who gave himself for us, that he might redeem us from all iniquity, and purify unto himself a peculiar people, zealous of good works."

Titus 2:13, 14

OLD ORDER
AMISH FARM
IN THE
KALONA COMMUNITY.

Photo by Joan Liffring Zug

C H A P T E R   O N E

Driving southwest along Iowa Highway 1 from Iowa City to Kalona, travelers can see the many farmyards containing buggies and other horse-drawn equipment. They might notice big, well-kept farmhouses and, in many instances, a small house located adjacent to a larger home. A closer look would reveal that no electricity or telephone lines were running from roadside poles to the houses or outbuildings.

If the visitors paused longer, they would undoubtedly see children playing: the little girls wearing long dark dresses, black prayer caps, long black stockings, and black oxfords; the young boys attired in dark solid-colored shirts and "broadfalls" trousers, with a buttoned front flap and held up by cloth suspenders.

A glimpse into one of the roomy farmhouses would reveal a busy farm wife bustling around her kitchen intent on baking, canning, and cooking to fullfill her family's needs. A small child might be playing beside her, and perhaps an older daughter would be helping with the innumerable domestic chores of washing, sewing, mending, and

2

The Old Order in Iowa

cleaning. Missing in the household would be any type of electrical appliance to lighten the homemaker's load. The work in this farm home is performed manually.

Past the farmyard and a short distance down the road, a farmer could be seen at work in his field. Again a brief glance would reflect an atypical Iowa scene. Missing would be the powerful modern tractor, the bags of commercial fertilizer, and the predominance of large fields of corn. Instead a bearded man, moving slowly through his field, would be using a team of horses to pull his old-fashioned farm equipment. A manure spreader might stand nearby, as this is the only type of fertilizer used by this particular agriculturist. The farmer would not be far from his house because his total landholdings would be around 100 acres.

This busy farm family belongs to a semiisolated, highly religious, and extremely successful utopian society called the Old Order Amish Mennonites. If travelers were to alter their course and drive north to

3

Hazleton in Buchanan County or head south to Milton in Van Buren County, the scenes would be much the same as those described along Highway 1 near Kalona.

The Old Order Amish Mennonites constitute Iowa's most distinctive religious minority. Descendants of early sixteenth century Mennonites, the Amish have successfully retained their religion and unchanging life-style for almost 300 years. All aspects of their daily lives—occupation, hours of work, means and destination of travel, choice of friends and mates, and economic habits—are determined by religious tenets and considerations. The continuation of Old World ways and religious doctrines has produced a highly distinctive minority characterized by belief in the superiority of agrarian life and desire to be isolated from influences outside their own group.

Made up of hundreds of smaller subgroups, the Mennonite Church is a huge, worldwide religious organization. The major groups in Iowa are the General Conference, (Old) Mennonites, Conservative Mennonites, Beachy Amish, and Old Order Amish; the General Conference is regarded as the most liberal. Within the framework of the Mennonite Church, the Old Order Amish are the most conservative element. The Beachy Amish first broke away from the Old Order in Pennsylvania

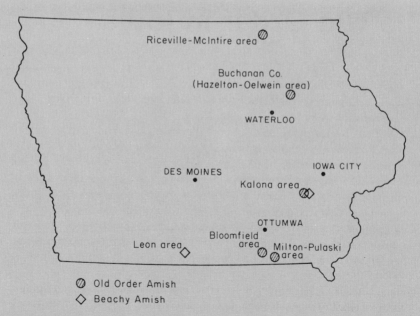

MAP 1. Old Order and Beachy Amish settlements in Iowa.

during the 1920s and are considered second in conservatism. Members of this group live in the Kalona and Leon areas.

The Amish first came to Iowa in the early 1840s and thus were among the first white settlers to move into the region. They located in Johnson and Washington counties and became prosperous agriculturists; this settlement constitutes the largest group of Old Order Amish in the state. In 1914 a small number left Kalona and moved to Buchanan County, believing the Kalona members had grown too worldly. This group has always been known as the Buchanan County settlement even though it centers around the community of Hazleton. They prospered and presently make up Iowa's second largest Old Order Amish settlement.

A third Old Order community in Iowa is located in the Milton-Pulaski area in the southeastern section of the state. Started in 1968 by five families from Buchanan County, the settlement has grown rapidly and six years after its inception contained about fifty families. The group at Milton believe that in the months and years ahead more Amish families will move there.

A small Old Order settlement is located west of Bloomfield. It began in the spring of 1971 and consisted originally of four related families, the elderly parents and three married sons. This group remained unchanged for almost three years; then in the spring of 1974 several additional Old Order families from Milton and from Clark, Missouri, joined the settlement. A new Iowa community containing six families was initiated in the spring of 1975 in the Riceville-McIntire area.

The Old Order in Iowa are part of a much larger Amish community spread throughout North and South America. The first Amish emigrated to the New World from Europe in the early 1700s, settling in southeastern Pennsylvania. From the beginning, they exhibited a high degree of geographical mobility. Spreading out from southeastern Pennsylvania, Amish soon moved into Maryland and other Middle Atlantic states as well as Ohio, Indiana, and other midwestern areas, always carrying with them their isolationist tendencies and strong religious beliefs.

The Iowa Old Order Amish live today much as their fellow Amishmen in other parts of the nation. Each settlement varies slightly from the others since the people respond to local conditions as well as to the desires and goals of their particular religious leaders. When traveling across the nation from a major Amish settlement like Lancaster County, Pennsylvania, through the Amish countryside in Ohio, Indiana, and Illinois, slight variations can be seen in the types of farm machinery,

MAP 2. Old Order and Beachy Amish settlements in the United States.

styles of clothing, and living patterns. The Old Order Amish in Lancaster County use modern farm machinery, believing it essential for their economic survival; in most other regions the Amish prefer old methods and machines. Within Iowa as well, slight differences exist between the three main communities. Some are as subtle as the width of a hat brim, or an inch or two difference in the length of a skirt; others are more obvious, such as the type of farm machinery used. Many Kalona Old Order use steel-wheeled tractors for field work, while the Buchanan County Amish use only horses. Overall, however, economic habits and life-styles are similar, regardless of location.

Yet another important consideration, both in Iowa and other sections of the country, is the Amish relationship to the American utopian movement. Because of their belief that they are "a peculiar people" and living a superior life, the Amish can be described as a utopian group. Unlike many utopians, however, the Amish do not desire to change or reform society around them. Their entire life-style is directed toward preserving or retaining the religious beliefs, economic patterns, and social structure they have experienced since their beginning. This commitment to the past also means that the Amish must be able to at least semiisolate themselves from non-Amish people and institutions. They have succeeded in perpetuating their beliefs and have become one of the most successful utopian societies in the world. The Hutterites, a communal religious organization with approximately

200 colonies located in the western United States and Canada, form another such group.

Also located in Iowa is a second highly distinctive religious minority known as the Society of True Inspiration or, as they are more popularly called, the Amana Colonies. Frequently travelers to the Amanas, believing they are visiting the Amish, will ask why they have not seen any horses or buggies driving around the villages. Although outward similarities exist between the two groups, there is no historical connection nor religious tie. Because the Amish are Mennonites their heritage goes back to Menno Simons, a religious reformer who lived in Europe during the sixteenth century. The Society of True Inspiration, with their seven villages located a short distance west of Iowa City, split off from the Lutheran Church in Germany in the early 1700s. Perhaps contributing to the misunderstanding that these groups are the same is the fact that before 1932 the Amana people lived in a communal, semiisolated fashion. They attempted to separate themselves from the outside world as much as possible and forbade their members to buy or use any modern conveniences such as the automobile. When they dropped the communal organization in 1932, interaction with outsiders greatly increased. The image of Amana before 1932 still lingers on and no doubt perpetuates the mistaken relationship between the two groups.

A LATER PORTRAIT OF THE
FIRST AMISH COUPLE TO BE
MARRIED IN THE KALONA COMMUNITY
IN THE EARLY 1840S.

CHAPTER TWO

Origin and Growth

Iowa's Old Order Amish Mennonites have a long and often tumultuous history. While the origins of the Mennonite Church are in the Swiss Anabaptist movement of the early 1500s, the group known as Amish began in the late 1600s. A strong difference of opinion existed among Mennonite groups regarding the practice of shunning or avoidance of excommunicated members. Some individuals like Jakob Ammann believed in total avoidance of sinful members, while others advocated a more moderate approach. The controversy eventually split the European Mennonite congregations into two groups and those that agreed with Ammann came to be known as Amish. In the early 1700s small numbers of Amish began to migrate to the American colonies, and a century later they had all either left Europe or had reunited with European Mennonite churches. Since settlement in the United States, they have experienced a number of schisms in their own society. Because of these numerous splits it is necessary when writing of the Amish to distinguish between the Old Order, the Conservative group, and more recently, the Beachy Amish.

EARLY SWISS ANABAPTISTS

Iowa's Old Order Amish trace their origins to the Swiss Anabaptists that originated in Switzerland during the time of the Protestant Reformation. Swiss reformer Ulrich Zwingli was prominently involved in development of the group. Born in the Swiss canton of St. Gall in 1484, Zwingli trained for the priesthood and then served in Glarus and Einsiedeln before moving to Zurich. During that

9

time he began to embrace the humanistic, reformist teachings of Erasmus, although remaining in the Roman Catholic Church and hoping fervently for internal reform. In 1519 he was appointed head pastor of Zurich. Later, when Zwingli learned of Martin Luther's excommunication, he realized the futility of reform from within the Church. In 1522 he left the priesthood but was reemployed as an evangelical pastor by the Zurich City Council.[1]

During this period of religious uncertainty, Zwingli had gathered around himself a number of young humanists and clergy who shared his religious thinking. This small band would later form the nucleus for the Swiss Anabaptist movement. After 1522 these followers became increasingly disillusioned with Zwingli as they were unable to persuade him to instigate several major religious reforms. Believing that their leader had given in to the conservatism of the Zurich authorities, the unhappy group called for the immediate abolition of the Mass because they believed it was not biblical. Zwingli rejected this demand as well as repudiating their thinking on the need for adult baptism based on the personal confession of faith. His followers still held with many of his earlier views, nevertheless, and began traveling from community to community holding Bible meetings. They attracted large audiences, and in some areas regular meetings were held. These steady participants began to call each other brother, marking the origin of the name Swiss Brethren.[2] However, ultimately a split did ensue between Zwingli and many of his disaffected followers—among them Conrad Grebel, Simon Stumpf, and Felix Manz—because of differences over the slowness and insufficiency of reform, infant baptism, a free church of voluntary believers, and the need for church discipline.[3]

In January 1525 Zwingli publicly debated with a number of his ex-followers on the topic of infant baptism. The Zurich City Council refused to accept his opponents' arguments and decreed instead that all infants must be baptized; furthermore, they ruled that Grebel and his associates should hold no more meetings. A few days later, however, the first Swiss Brethren congregation of the Reformation days was formed when Grebel's Zurich group organized a church and baptized fifteen people, thus beginning the Anabaptist movement. Following this action, members experienced severe persecution and some leaders were imprisoned. In March 1526 Zurich officials pronounced the death sentence for anyone who had been rebaptized.[4]

The term "Anabaptist," a Greek word meaning "rebaptizer," was introduced and used by enemies of the Swiss Brethren because of the criminal connotation of the word. The enemies of Anabaptism were no doubt basing their actions on the fact that from Justinian's time (A.D.

529) the imperial law code labeled rebaptism a heresy punishable by death. The totally evil meaning of the name made these people at once subject to condemnation and execution. The persecuted group rejected the name Anabaptist claiming that infant baptism was not baptism at all; instead they believed the sacrament rested on confession of faith and commitment to discipleship by the candidate.[5]

The organization used no standard name since it was not a unified movement, but identification as Anabaptists persisted. One group adopted the name of their leader Jakob Hutter and came to be known as Hutterites. In response to persecution in Switzerland, these brethren had fled to Moravia where, faced with extreme poverty, they had established a common household. They then adopted the community of goods principle and became known as the Hutterite Brethren. The remaining members who did not ascribe to the communal principle retained the name Swiss Brethren since they were of Swiss origin, although they lived in other places as well as in Switzerland.[6] The Swiss Brethren suffered severe persecution which forced their members out of Zurich and St. Gall; Bern then became their main stronghold. From there they spread to northern Switzerland, southern Germany, and Moravia.[7]

Even though there was no unified Anabaptist movement in the early 1500s, a common ideology did develop. The name itself revealed belief in adult baptism because of conviction that the church should be a voluntary association of believers. "Repent, believe and be baptized" was the biblical decree, and since infants were incapable of this behavior, they could not meet the qualifications for membership in a voluntary church. At the same time this belief set the Anabaptists against the concept of the state church, which advocated that all people should be baptized at infancy. Anabaptist beliefs required that each member experience a "conscious change (rebirth) of life and intent" through this faith in Christ. The resulting free, voluntary association of those who confessed their faith in Christ formed a community of true believers.[8]

The Anabaptists also believed in separation from the world and nonviolence. Members were admonished to live "nonconformed" to the world, a belief that demanded that they dress simply and without signs of pride. They were also to manifest this religious conviction by refusing to serve in any public offices. Even more radical for its day was the belief in nonresistance or nonviolence. Refusing to bear arms, Anabaptists asserted that Christians should not fight with swords but with their religious faith and commitment.

The emergence of the Anabaptists reflected a general reorganization of religious groups in the early sixteenth century. On the right was the Roman Catholic Church whose officials opposed any real change in religious doctrine. More to the center of the spectrum was Martin Luther, rejecting some of the Church's teachings but retaining many of the major beliefs. To the left of center was the Reformed Party led by Zwingli. This group, although certainly more liberal than Luther, still believed in the tie between church and state. On the extreme left were the Anabaptists, rejecting many of the tenets of the Reformers and wanting complete separation of church and state. Thus the beliefs of the Anabaptists provided adequate reasons for the dominant religious groups not only to reject them but to view them as a serious threat to the established order.

While the Anabaptist movement was spreading throughout northern Switzerland, southern Germany, and Moravia, an independent group was developing in the Netherlands. Led initially by Melchior Hoffman, a follower of Martin Luther, and later by two brothers, Obbe and Dirk Philips, the group came to be called Obbenites. The doctrines they taught were similar to those of the Swiss Brethren. After 1536 Menno Simons, a former Roman Catholic priest, became the Obbenite leader. Simons worked in Holland, northwestern Germany, and during the final years of his life, in Holstein. Reflecting his strong influence, the Obbenites came to be known as Mennonites or followers of Menno. Gradually the term was applied to those Swiss Brethren in southern Germany and Switzerland who had embraced the same religious doctrines. The Mennonites prospered in Holland, and eventually many members migrated to England, East and West Prussia, the Ukraine and Crimea in southern Russia, and then to North America. Those who remained in the Netherlands eventually won religious toleration and many later became members of the merchant class.[10]

During these times of peaceful prosperity, Mennonite members were able to maintain closer contact with one another as well as to establish relations among congregations. Religious leaders from southern Germany, northern Germany, Moravia, and Switzerland were periodically able to confer, and a sense of unity gradually developed. With the gathering of churchmen from different parts of Europe, however, it became apparent that members could not agree on the application of a major rule, the *Meidung* or ban. Under this rule the Mennonite Church could excommunicate any person who had committed a serious crime; there the consensus ended, however, as many different views existed on how the ban should be implemented.[11]

In 1554 Mennonite leaders from northern Germany and the

Netherlands held a conference in Wismar, where they adopted a church discipline that included a statement on enforcement of the ban. This statement supported the views of Menno Simons, who attended the Wismar meeting and believed along with other participants that shunning (as the application of the ban came to be called) should be enforced severely, even to the point of a husband or wife refusing to continue domestic relations with a guilty spouse. Church leaders from Switzerland, southern Germany, and Moravia, protesting what they referred to as the Wismar rule, believed the statement was too strict and refused to accept that interpretation. During the late sixteenth century and throughout the seventeenth century the Mennonite Church was unable to reach agreement on a uniform application of the *Meidung;* the northern members enforced strict shunning, while the Swiss Brethren applied it only to spiritual fellowship and communion.[12]

BIRTH OF THE AMISH

One elder who took a most radical position regarding shunning was Jakob Ammann of Erlenbach, Canton of Bern, Switzerland. Believing that the churches in Switzerland were lax in their enforcement of the *Meidung,* Ammann, acting as a self-appointed authority, visited the Swiss pastors and inquired of each what his policy was in regard to this practice. If the pastor answered that he did indeed strictly enforce the *Meidung,* Ammann proceeded to ask two additional controversial questions: Did the pastor believe that true-hearted persons would be saved? Did he believe that persons who were guilty of telling a falsehood should be excommunicated? The "true-hearted" or "noble-hearted" were defined as persons who sympathized with the Mennonites and shared many of their views but did not openly join the group, although aiding them during times of persecution. However, this did not qualify them to be "saved." Ammann expected and demanded explicit answers on both questions, negative for the first and affirmative for the second, and showed extreme disfavor if a pastor answered them incorrectly. As well as his insistence that the Swiss Brethren strictly enforce the *Meidung,* Ammann also advocated that there should be uniformity in dress among the Mennonites and that beards should not be trimmed. He had earlier introduced the practice of footwashing into the communion service.[13]

One of the Swiss elders confronted by Ammann was Hans Reist of the Emmental, Canton of Bern, who disagreed on the matter of not eating with those who had been excommunicated. In supporting his position, Reist stated, "What one eats is no sin; Christ also ate with publicans and sinners." This unsatisfactory response as well as disagreement on other matters angered Ammann and led him to attempt to unify the entire Swiss Mennonite ministry on three issues: (1) acceptance of the strict interpretation of application of the *Meidung,* (2) refusal to accept the teaching that true-hearted persons would be saved, and (3) insistence that members admit that attending state church services was wrong. Following the second unsuccessful attempt, seven of Ammann's followers held a meeting that can be viewed as the first Amish gathering. This action in 1693 marked the actual division of the parent group into Mennonites and Amish. Ammann then excommunicated Reist and several other ministers.[14]

Even though three issues were included in the controversial meetings and encounters between Ammann and other Swiss Mennonite officials, Mennonite Church authorities believe that the shunning or *Meidung* issue was the major if not the full cause of the split. Following the break, several attempts were made by church authorities to reconcile the two wings, but no agreement could be reached. Ammann, actively teaching that the interpretation of this group was the only correct one, continued to place opposing ministers under the ban, and eventually all Mennonite congregations in Switzerland, Alsace, and south Germany had divided into factions. Later, as a conciliatory effort, the Amish placed themselves under the *Meidung* to indicate that they would accept the same treatment they had meted out to those members not in agreement with them. However, at subsequent conferences they would not yield on the strict observance of shunning, and this made a complete and lasting compromise impossible.[15]

EARLY AGRICULTURAL HISTORY

During their European history the persecution suffered by the Amish sometimes took the form of banishment from land ownership. At other times the Amish could not even rent land. Frequently they were able to secure only marginal or mountainous land and sometimes paid special taxes and higher rents simply to be accepted as tenants. Under the pressure of these adverse conditions, the Amish quickly discarded old, traditional farming methods and devised new ways to build up the fertility of the poor soil. Their very existence depended on willingness and ability to experiment. Because of these economic and social pressures they became the first in central Europe to try new methods of fertilization, cattle feeding, and fodder cultivation.[16]

Crop rotation was another innovation the Amish devised in their attempts to offset low crop yields resulting from poor land. Importing clover from Holland, they first adapted it to the Palatine area and after several decades were recognized as excellent clover farmers. Clover improved the soil, producing more feed for stock and thus more manure for fertilizer. This marked the initiation of the four-year crop rotation system the Amish continue to use today. In the Palatinate this practice checked the problem of soil destruction, gradually improving the economy of the entire region. Thus early in their history the European Amish applied innovations in agriculture that frequently improved farming techniques and crops.[17]

A second characteristic was the sharing of new agricultural information. Amish congregations kept in close contact and members passed along new farming methods that could be tried and evaluated by other church people. In this way they developed a broader understanding of established practices as well as new methods. This gave them a decided advantage over peasant farmers who knew little or nothing about techniques other than their own.[18]

Even with superior farming methods and rapid agricultural adaptability it is doubtful if the Amish could have continued in Europe. Because it was difficult to purchase land, they were never able to form primary community groupings and thus did not live in compact settlements. Faced with periodic persecution, many Amish settled wherever they were given asylum and then rented or purchased property. As a result each Amish family was a "social unit unto itself," unlike their later settlements in the New World. Moreover, geographical distances prevented much interaction among large numbers of families. Even in dress the European Amish did not set themselves apart, as they dressed in a manner similar to their rural, non-Amish neighbors. It was therefore difficult to remain separate and be unaffected by the world about them.[19] Faced with many problems as a result of these restrictions as well as continued sporadic religious persecution, the Amish began to seek a totally new area for future settlement.

NEW WORLD MIGRATION

The first Amish came to America in the early 1700s in response to William Penn's invitation to settle his colony; within a few years many families had moved to Lancaster County. Settlement in the region proved a wise decision because of excellent farming conditions; fertile soil, gentle rolling terrain, adequate rainfall, moderate temperatures, and a long growing season all aided the Amish. In later years the area also proved advantageous as excellent market facilities developed for their products. Applying to fertile Pennsylvania soil their time-proven agricultural techniques, the Amish quickly became known as superior family-sized farmers.[20]

From the beginning of their Pennsylvania settlement, the Amish exhibited a high degree of mobility. Spreading out from southeastern Pennsylvania, Amish soon moved into Maryland, Delaware, Ohio, Indiana, and Illinois and by the early 1840s were among the first settlers moving into the territory of Iowa. The earliest Iowa Amish were from Ohio and settled in Lee County. A few years later other Ohio Amish moved into Washington Township in Johnson County. Like their Pennsylvania forefathers, Iowa Amish selected an excellent location. Southeast Iowa offered adequate rainfall, fertile soil, sufficient timber, and a growing season of approximately 170 days.[21] The agricultural practices that had served them so well both in Europe and in the eastern United States were applied to southeastern Iowa, bringing them the same economic prosperity experienced previously.

AMISH SCHISMS IN THE UNITED STATES

By the early 1860s it had become apparent that the wide dispersement of Amish communities throughout the eastern United States would result in some variation in life-styles and economic practices. To provide a means for reconciling differences arising from this mobility as well as for regular consultation, an annual General Ministers' Conference was started in 1862. Many problems were resolved but many remained, and the conference disbanded after 1878.[22]

The wide dispersement also supported the development of several different schools of thought among the Amish regarding general life-style and separation from the world. Before 1850 it was necessary only to use the name Amish when speaking of the followers of Jakob Ammann. After 1850, however, several major schisms occurred which splintered the group into numerous factions. The first originated around 1850 when some members began to feel that Amish brethren were growing too worldly. Gradually over the next twenty years, this group came to be called the Old Order as they resisted further changes in their life-style, rejected separate meeting houses for religious services, stressed plain clothing, and insisted on a rural way of life. The opposing group, sometimes called the progressive element but more commonly referred to as Amish Mennonites, organized three church districts after 1882. These were the Eastern Amish Mennonites, the Indiana-Michigan Amish Mennonites, and the West District Amish Mennonites. Later all three groups merged with more liberal Mennonite conferences and dropped the word Amish from their name. A third group included several schisms—occurring in Illinois, Indiana, and Ohio between 1865 and 1875—that led to the formation of the Evangelical Mennonite Church (formerly Defenseless Mennonites) and the Central Conference.[23] A fourth group that developed in 1912 could be described as in-between since they did not accept either the Old Order or Amish Mennonite positions and therefore organized the Conservative Amish Mennonite group. They particularly did not want to stay with the Old Order since they desired to engage in evangelism and hold Sunday school. In 1954 they too dropped the word Amish from their conference name.[24]

Between 1923 and 1927 the most recent major split occurred when a group called the Beachy Amish broke away from the Old Order. In Iowa one congregation is located at Kalona and one at Leon. These groups differ from the Old Order in that their members may use electricity and telephones, own automobiles, and hold their services in a separate church building. Some confusion results from the variety of names that various congregations use. In Indiana, for example, the Beachy Amish are called the Burkholder Amish after their Nappanee, Indiana, group leader. In Lancaster County, Pennsylvania, the Beachy group was referred to as the John A. Stoltzfus Church or the Weavertown Amish.[25] Although the Beachy Amish now number over 4,000 throughout the United States, they have not yet organized into a formal church conference.

Thus beginning in the 1860s several general factions can be discerned in Amish society. The first and most conservative was the Old Order; second, at that time, were the more liberal Amish Mennonites such as the Stuckey Amish from Woodford and Bureau counties in Illinois, who established a church in Pocahontas County; and third were the middle-of-the-road churches that rejected both the most conservative and most liberal elements. However, the distinctions typically associated with the original Amish such as the plain dress, the horse and buggy mode of transportation, and the general rejection of worldliness are characteristic only of the Old Order.[26]

EARLY AMISH SETTLEMENTS IN IOWA

Before 1900 the Amish established settlements in widely separated areas of the state. Some remain as thriving communities, while others are now extinct leaving little if any physical trace of their existence.

The first Amish settlement in Iowa was in the early 1840s in Lee County. The Amish had purchased land once contained in the Half-Breed Tract, an area set aside for half-breed members of the Sac and Fox Indian tribes. Later when many Indians sold their holdings, there was much confusion over land titles. Uncertain about the legality of their land deeds and opposed to taking the matter to court, the Amish simply sold their land and moved to other communities. The Lee County settlement reached its peak in 1855 with fifty members, but following that date many families began to move away. Some moved to Davis County, others to Henry County, and some moved out of the state. By 1870 the community was nonexistent.[27]

Also during the 1840s Amish settlements were made in eastern Jefferson and western Henry counties. A few years later they spread into southeastern Washington County. Following the major split that resulted in the formation of the Old Order, the Henry County churches became known simply as Amish, later changing the name to Amish Mennonites. This also applied to the Washington County group. In 1893 these Amish joined the General Conference Mennonites, the most liberal faction of the Mennonite Church.[28]

In 1846 the first Amish moved into Johnson County. Like earlier settlers in Lee and Henry counties, most of these people were from Ohio. Following the example of other early pioneers, they lived in log cabins and made furniture from the basswood found nearby. The inevitable pioneer affliction of fever and ague caused considerable suffering among these people, and when reports of this illness filtered back East, the flow of migration ceased for a few years. In the spring of 1850, however, the situation appeared changed and once more the Amish began moving westward into Johnson County.[29]

All Amish communities experienced some dissension, but the Johnson County group appeared to face an extraordinarily high number of disagreements regarding practices and policies. Following the initial organization, several families who believed that the rules were too liberal moved into the community. A minor but illustrative detail concerned the use of colored or decorated dishes. The leader of this faction, Assistant Elder Joseph Keim, believed that such utensils reflected pride and should not be used. Eventually Keim and Deacon John Mishler started holding services in their home in 1863, apart from the main group. Four ministers were brought in from other states to help smooth out the difficulties, and although they did succeed in ending the separate church services, a number of members eventually left the district.[30]

Around 1863 the Johnson County Amish divided into two church districts because of increased membership; those who lived in Washington Township and in Iowa County belonged to the Deer Creek church while those in Sharon Township and in Northern Washington County established the second district. In 1877 Johnson County officials found it necessary once more to create new districts because of additional members; the Sharon District was divided into North Sharon and South Sharon churches and the Deer Creek District became the Upper Deer Creek and Lower Deer Creek districts.[31] Many attempts were made to arbitrate the frequent disagreements between conservative and liberal factions, but not all the dissensions were eliminated. As with countless other Amish groups, the Johnson County settlement was faced with the decision as to whether they should accept modern inventions like the automobile and the telephone. In 1912 the Kalona Lower Deer Creek church was strongly affected by a division of opinion among its membership over the use of the telephone. Eventually the group split into two factions over the issue.[32]

During the mid-1800s Davis County had a sizable Amish settlement. Some Amish families that had settled previously in Lee County moved near Pulaski in the 1850s along with families from Canada, Ohio, and Indiana. By 1860 almost fifty Amish families had purchased land in Davis County but had no church because they did not have a minister. The coming of the Civil War expedited the matter of church organization because the elders wanted to aid their young men in securing exemptions from military service. They invited Elder Jacob Swartzendruber of Johnson County to assist them. Being conservative in his views, this elder insisted that before formal organization the Davis County Amishmen should make certain changes in their appearance such as growing beards and cutting their hair in a particular fashion. Rejecting these suggestions, they later invited two Indiana ministers to come and thereafter successfully organized a congregation. In 1863 they purchased land for a cemetery and for a church that they completed in 1866. As more Amish families settled in the area, a larger church building was constructed in 1885. Originally the members had adopted the name Amish Mennonite, later dropping the word Amish.[33] This church now belongs to the General Conference Mennonite group and is active in the Pulaski area.[34]

During the decade of the 1890s the Amish initiated three settlements in northwestern Iowa. In 1892 several families purchased land around Manson in Calhoun County because it was cheaper than land in eastern Iowa. Furthermore, with ample land available, the Amish could logically assume that their children would also be able to obtain farms in the vicinity, thus keeping the family units together. Referring to themselves as Amish Mennonites, they organized a church in 1897. Also attracted to this settlement was the group called Stuckey Amish, which wanted to organize its own church but did not have sufficient members. They attended the Amish Mennonite church but did not join because the men did not want to shave off their mustaches and the women resisted wearing bonnets instead of hats. About a decade after their first church was built, the congregation erected one within Manson itself. As new inventions like the automobile came into use, the Manson congregation quickly adopted them, reflecting the progressive tenor of the group.[35]

Wright and Pocahontas counties marked the location of two other Amish churches in northwestern Iowa. In Wright County the congregation encountered difficulties over a member who had fallen into disrepute with his former Old Order Amish group in Johnson County. Rather than make a requested confession to his Johnson County church, he had departed. His appearance in the Wright County community and subsequent contrariness produced a devastating schism within that congregation, where his brother, Solomon Swartzendruber, was bishop. As a result of this split, members gradually began to move away and the church finally dissolved.[36]

In 1897 and 1898 a few Amish Mennonite and Stuckey Amish families settled in Pocahontas County. Remaining small in number, the group conducted Sunday school but never organized into a church district. Within a few years families became increasingly afraid that their children would marry non-Mennonites and so began moving away to join better established congregations in other parts of the state.[37]

SUMMARY

Originating in Europe and emigrating to the United States, the Amish have for almost 300 years successfully maintained their early religious beliefs and have conformed very little to societal pressures. Their migration to the United States ensured that they could continue as "a peculiar people." In the New World they found the land they so desperately needed for compact community settlements; they discovered that religious freedom was indeed a reality; they also soon realized that when faced with schisms within their groups, it was possible for dissenters to detach themselves, move to another section of the country, and start afresh by implementing their particular principles. Thus from the beginning of Amish society, mobility has played a key role.

Another major consideration is that as a group in this country the Amish took on an outward identity they did not have in the Old World. In America they began to wear a common, distinctive dress and so developed a badge of recognition. As society evolved around them, they resisted all change, thus becoming increasingly obvious, more conservative, and seemingly more "peculiar." It is doubtful, had they remained in Europe, that they would have developed the separatist tendencies so vital to their success.

Their Iowa experience also points out that not all Amish communities survive. This same pattern is being repeated in the neighboring state of Missouri. Many new Amish communities have been established there since the 1960s and some such as the Fortuna group no longer exist.

THE CHURCH BENCH WAGON IN THE
FOREGROUND INDICATES THAT
CHURCH WILL BE HELD AT THIS
OLD ORDER AMISH HOME NEXT SUNDAY.

CHAPTER THREE

Religious Practices

Early Sunday morning in an Old Order Amish community a long string of black buggies can be seen moving slowly down the road, all headed for a particular farmstead. This procession means that it is church meeting time for the Plain People. This particular day is an important one to the Amish as they come together to worship with other members of their faith. The time will be spent singing, praying, listening to preaching, and doing a great deal of visiting. Not only will religious matters be dealt with during the morning but community matters as well. However, Sunday is not the only day when the Amish are concerned with their church; they live in a world shaped totally by their religious convictions. Their tenets decree that they live among other Amish, reject modernism in any form, and separate themselves from the world. The basic community organization is the church district, and within that body the bishop is the religious and secular leader. Because of the all-pervasive qualities of religious life, an Amish member is constantly reminded, spiritually or physically, of his or her convictions.

AMISH RELIGIOUS BELIEFS

The major religious beliefs of the Old Order Amish are set down in the *Dortrecht Confession of Faith,* a document written at Dortrecht, Holland, in 1632. The confession contains eighteen articles that cover all the basic religious tenets of the Old Order Amish (see Appendix C). Most important are the Anabaptist principle of adult baptism, separation from the world, nonresistance and refusal to bear arms, and

23

refusal to take an oath. To the Amish, adult baptism means that the individual is making the choice to believe rather than parents as in the case of infant baptism. Separation from the world is supported by two Bible verses: "And be not conformed to this world: but ye transformed by the renewing of your mind, that ye may prove what is that good, and acceptable, and perfect, will of God" (Romans 12:2); and "Be ye not unequally yoked together with unbelievers: for what fellowship hath righteousness with unrighteousness? and what communion hath light with darkness?" (II Corinthians 6:14). Nonresistance means that Amishmen will never bear arms nor retaliate when treated in a hostile manner. Regarding their refusal to take oaths (except to God), they have sometimes been requested to testify in court, which requires the swearing of an oath. Some have been able to solve this dilemma by asking permission to state, "I affirm" rather than "I swear."[1]

Articles are also included in the *Dortrecht Confession* covering behavior in the areas of shunning, communion, and matrimony. The remainder of the rules governing conduct are usually imposed by local church districts; these are unwritten and typically of a less comprehensive nature. If the Amish members obey the rules of the church and live in "full fellowship" or in harmony with their religion, they have hope of salvation or *lebendige Hoffnung*.[2] To state that they are assured of salvation, however, is considered vain and boastful.

THE CHURCH DISTRICT

Every Old Order Amish community is divided into church districts that provide the basic form of religious, political, and social organization for Amish society. Each district contains from fifteen to thirty families who live in close proximity to one another. The most obvious need for establishment of districts is apparent when all families within a given district come together at a member's home for their Sunday morning church service. Given their horse and buggy mode of transportation, they must live fairly close so that minimum time is spent traveling. The number of families within each church district must also be limited because even though large homes are commonplace, they can rarely accommodate more than 100 people.

Since the Amish have no statewide or national religious organization or religious leaders, each church district is largely autonomous in matters that affect members, whether religious, political, or economic in nature. The choice of religious leaders is totally in the hands of the church district membership. Once selected, the highest religious official, the bishop, then in the fullest sense becomes the leader of his people. The rules as defined by the bishop are unwritten but well understood by all members of the church district. Assisting the bishop in all his duties are two or more ministers and sometimes one or two deacons, also selected by the church district membership. Amishmen must be married before they are eligible for these positions.

Church services are held every other Sunday and every family member eagerly looks forward to that day. The young people enjoy Sunday because there is less work to do and they can be with their friends. To the adults the day represents a change of routine as they come together to worship, but it also provides an opportunity to visit family members and friends. On Sunday morning everyone is eager to finish their chores so they can get ready for church. All have special clothes they wear for this and other special events such as the Sunday night sing and weddings and funerals. Amish women wear cape dresses distinguished by a triangular piece of cloth usually made from the same fabric as the dress, that is worn over the shoulders like a shawl and comes to a point near the waistline. Their outfit also includes an apron, typically made from the same material as the dress. The unmarried girls wear the same style of dress but have white capes and aprons and cross the capes differently so that the ends are tucked into the back of their dresses. Young boys wear black trousers, white shirts, and long open vests. The men have a special jacket, called a wamus, that they wear on Sunday and for other special occasions. Another jacket, a *Mutze,* is worn only when they preach.[3]

When it is time to leave for church, several buggies are hitched up to accommodate all the family members and everyone sets out for the farm where the service is being held. The drive is leisurely since the family has allowed plenty of time. If they find themselves behind another buggy, they remain there as it would be considered rude to pass another on the way to church. In winter the host finds room in his barns for the horses. If the service is being held at a neighbor's farm, the closest families will walk rather than hitch up the buggies. One Amish boy of four or five provided a particularly happy sight as he trudged down the road, obviously enjoying himself and his surroundings, with his large black hat resting on his ears, his white shirt with sleeves just a little too long, his black trousers with pant legs just a bit too short, his vest flapping open and shut as he bounced along, and as a final touch to his Sunday outfit — no shoes, just chubby, tanned, bare feet!

As the families arrive at their destination, the men gather in the farmyard, eager to discuss such common topics of interest as the crops, the weather, and any community events that have taken place. The women are involved in caring for the younger children and helping the hostess prepare the food, but they also have considerable time to socialize among themselves. The attendance at church is usually 100 percent, since the only acceptable reason for absence is illness or being out of the community. Every week in the *Budget* (a widely distributed newspaper covering Amish affairs) the different reporters, or scribes, list members who missed church because of illness, usually adding a comment about their health. When a member has recovered sufficiently to be present at church, this is also noted in the *Budget.*

The family hosting the Sunday service spends considerable time preparing for the event. They clean house thoroughly and prepare the traditional foods; typically the same family will host two consecutive services rather than one. On Saturday the furniture is moved out of the living room and dining room or pushed back against the walls, and backless benches are placed throughout the two main rooms. Sometimes it is necessary to place benches in the kitchen and main bedroom as well. Special wagons carry the benches from house to house, and the presence of the bench wagon in a yard is a sure sign that Sunday services will be held at that farm.

At 9:30 A.M. everyone assembles in the main rooms. The men sit in one area and the women in another with the bishop and the ministers between. Three songs are sung by the congregation without any musical accompaniment, while the ministers and the bishop have a meeting and decide who is going to preach the sermon. Frequently the singing has a sad, mournful quality, and it may take as long as twenty minutes to sing a single hymn. Following the singing one of the religious leaders presents a short sermon, a prayer, and a scripture reading. The main sermon is then presented and frequently lasts an hour and a half. The preaching is done primarily out of the New Testament, as the Amish use the Old Testament only twice a year. The man presenting the main sermon has selected a text but has not formally prepared his talk. Throughout the sermon, he will reiterate the text and use many Bible verses, but the Amish stress that the speaker does not prepare his remarks ahead of time. If a visiting bishop is present, he may be asked to give the main sermon. If the small children become fussy during the service, the hostess may pass a bowl of crackers to quiet them, followed by a glass of water that is also passed from child to child. A benediction, announcements, and the singing of a closing hymn end the service around noon, and the hostess serves a hearty lunch. Amish women traditionally serve bread, cold meats, butter, jams, jellies, pickles, pie, and coffee.[4]

The bishop and ministers hold a council after the service to make certain that the man preaching covered everything he had intended to say. Some Amishmen have reputations as excellent speakers, and invitations to attend church service have been extended with the comment, "Come and hear our bishop preach. He will make your hair stand up on your head!"[5]

The Sunday morning services also provide an opportunity for church members to discuss topics that are important but not totally of a religious nature. Because of the autonomy of each district, this meeting permits members to discuss what to non-Amish people would be secular matters. In this sense the church district becomes the unit of local government for the Plain People. Following the formal church service, discussions will be held regarding problems of the young people, community events such as frolics, and the health of certain members, to mention only a few topics that might naturally arise. A group of Kalona Old Order visited the State Highway Commission in Ames requesting that highway officials add ten-foot shoulders to each side of Iowa Highway 22 between Kalona and Riverside. The Amish contended that the absence of shoulders made buggy travel dangerous in that area.[6] This topic was discussed among the different congregations, and provisions were made for the delegation to travel to Ames. The Amish use their church meetings as discussion forums for all matters that confront them as well as to determine their collective stand on important issues.

Although the Buchanan County Old Order do not do so, beginning in April and continuing through early fall, the Kalona Old Order church districts hold Sunday school in a building provided for this purpose. These sessions are held on the Sundays that fall between the regular church services. The practice is discontinued in the fall because there is no way to shelter the horses during cold weather. When Sunday school classes begin in the spring, members start through the New Testament chapter by chapter. They study and discuss each one and if they do not complete all the Scriptures by the end of the sessions, they pick up the following spring where they had left off in the fall and continue until they do finish. During these sessions Amish youngsters also are taught German and catechism.[7]

On the Sundays when church services are held, the young people reassemble at the same home for their evening service, the "Sunday night sing." The host parents are present but usually do not participate in the activities. The sing is the major social function for the

SUNDAY SCHOOL
IN SESSION NEAR
KALONA.

Photo by Joan Liffring Zug

adolescents. It provides an opportunity for single youths of sixteen and older to engage in courtship activities as well as to participate in social activities geared to their age level. The evening is spent primarily singing religious songs, but it is also expected that there will be a great deal of laughing, joking, storytelling, teasing, and all the general antics of young people together in a social setting. Although many come alone or with older brothers or sisters, it is customary for the boys and girls to pair off during the evening, with the young men taking their girl friends home.

CHURCH LEADERS

In the hierarchy of each church district there is a bishop; two or more ministers; and sometimes one or more deacons, occasionally

referred to as elders. These religious leaders have had no formal training nor are they paid for their services. In a newly established church district, the leadership may be provided by the bishop and ministers of an established district until the new congregation is able to select its own religious men. The bishop is the major figure in the church district. If a decision is needed regarding an Amish family that may wish to move into the community, the bishop decides if they are acceptable. The bishop is also responsible for decisions regarding the use of certain types of farm equipment such as tractors. He administers such sacraments of the church as communion and baptism; performs marriages; and when the need arises, excommunicates sinful members. The bishop is responsible for securing the opinion of his members whenever it is necessary to seek unanimity among them over a serious church matter such as shunning and reinstatement. In these matters, counsel is provided by the entire church membership as the bishop takes a voice vote among the members. The final decision about the conduct of the membership, however, is in the bishop's hands, and he ultimately determines the major policies for his district. If a serious matter persists which local leaders seem unable to resolve, the bishop of another district may be called in to provide mediation.

To function effectively, the bishop must be a man of compassion and commitment. Because of the integrated nature of Amish society, he not only must tend to the religious concerns of his people but must also be concerned with their mental and physical needs. If a couple begins to have mother-in-law problems, they come to their bishop. He counsels them as well as the mother-in-law, hoping to open avenues for discussion and to erase some of the friction and misunderstanding. When a young wife is unable physically and mentally to cope with her many responsibilities of child care and running the household, the young couple go to see their bishop. The wife may eventually seek psychiatric help, but the bishop is involved with the couple every step of the way. If an Amishman becomes too worldly in his associations with non-Amish people, the bishop must seek out the man and talk with him about the dangers inherent in such behavior. In all these relationships, the bishop must have great patience. He must listen, counsel, persuade, or admonish and if the members refuse to heed his advice he must firmly rebuke them. Only if there is extreme unwillingness to comply with the church rules or to repent and come back into the group will the bishop raise the issue of shunning with the entire church district membership. Underneath his patience and persuasive powers the bishop must remain resolute in upholding the church rules. His firmness is of paramount importance, for in the final analysis he is the main purveyor and perpetuator of the Amish faith.

The Amish do not choose a bishop hastily, and often a church district will be without for one or two years until consensus is reached that the time is right for selection. The membership is well aware of the strong influence of the bishop within the community and realize that the position is demanding in terms of time and energy. Moreover, the lack of formal training for religious leadership means that the members must examine each candidate carefully because they cannot rely upon any outside certification such as a college degree or seminary training to help them determine his fitness for this particular role. Each adult Amishman views his possible selection as bishop as a great responsibility, but one that he must accept if called upon. If selected, he will feel no personal pride but will humbly ask God's help and promise the congregation that he will try to do God's will. The election of a bishop is regarded as a major event and is usually attended by bishops and ministers from the other Old Order church districts within the community and perhaps religious leaders from other settlements as well. The method of selection may vary slightly from community to community, but generally is a combination of what the Amish consider to be first a choice by man and then a choice by God.

Only ordained ministers are eligible to become bishops. In the Kalona area each baptised member of the congregation has a vote. A visiting bishop and the church district ministers will be in a small, separate room, and each member of the congregation will pass by and cast a vote. Each minister receiving two votes (in some communities the minimum number is three) is a candidate. The visiting bishop then places a piece of paper in a hymnbook next to the hymn, ''The Song of Praise.'' Then on a table at the front of the room he places the same number of hymnbooks as there are candidates, including the one containing the paper; all books are similar in binding and size. One by one the names of the candidates are called out. The first comes forward, selects a book, and returns to his seat. The visiting bishop then steps forward, takes the book, and opens it to the proper place. If it contains the slip of paper, that man is the chosen one. If not, the process is repeated until the correct book is selected. The Amish feel that they help in the selection because they all vote, but then it is up to God to direct the final selection of the right man. Often the man selected feels that he has received ''the call.'' One bishop stated that when he was called to select his book, he looked down and could see right through the book to the slip of paper inside. He believed that it was God's will that he had been selected.[8]

Deacons and ministers are nominated by the general membership and then selected by lot if there is more than one nomination for each position. In some communities the position of deacon is not filled and his traditional duties are handled either by the bishop or by one of the ministers.

Ministers provide the major assistance for the bishop, both on Sunday morning and throughout the week, and alternate with him in presenting the sermon. Included in the charge that a minister takes at the time of ordination is the stipulation that he be able to stand before the congregation without book or notes. He also assists the bishop in serving communion. Since the Amish believe that the Bible is the ''word of God,'' they rely heavily on the Scriptures for prayers and sermons. The minister is responsible for reciting biblical passages and then expanding on them as the basis for the morning service. He is selected by the congregation for his knowledge of the Scriptures and his ability to interpret their meaning clearly and with vigor.

The deacon is chosen by the church district to assist the bishop and ministers in both religious and secular matters. The deacon may be asked by the bishop to travel about the district and report back on such matters as backsliding. He may also determine if a young couple who have been courting and desire to be married have the approval of the parents. If so, a wedding date is set and the event announced in church two weeks before the marriage is to take place. For many years it was customary to perform weddings in the fall, following completion of the harvest, but Amish weddings now are held throughout the year. At the time the deacon is ordained, he makes a pledge to ''care for widows and orphans and receive alms and give them out with the counsel of the church. . . .'' 9

Bishops, ministers, and deacons are appointments for life which carry over from one district to another as long as the communities are in full fellowship with one another. Under extreme conditions, however, the bishop or other religious leaders can be ''silenced,'' which means they are deprived of their traditional responsibilities. If an ordained person plans to move to a new community, there usually must be some prior approval by the membership of the settlement because, once there, he will take an active part in the religious life. It is generally known throughout the various Amish communities what position the different bishops have taken on important issues, and each is viewed in a particular light depending on his conservative or liberal stand.

The major area of difference among Old Order Amish communities is their interpretation of ''worldliness,'' which reflects the dominant convictions of the church district membership but is also strongly reinforced and in some cases created by the views of the bishop and to a lesser extent by those of the ministers and deacons. Because of these variations in interpretation each Amish community has a distinct flavor and reputation. To one bishop it may be worldly to allow men's hat brims to be less than four inches in width, but to another a three-inch brim may be acceptable. One bishop may reject the use of propane gas appliances while another may feel this is acceptable. In general, the degree of worldliness permitted is evident in many ways. Typically, the more conservative community will have less contact with non-Amish people in both business and social events; many times young people will not be allowed to work for outsiders. The degree of conservatism is even reflected in the manner in which the Amish sing their hymns on Sunday morning; the more conservative the church district, the longer it takes to sing each stanza. In communities where there are several church districts, religious leaders remain in close contact and hold regular meetings to discuss common problems.

BAPTISM AND COMMUNION

A member is baptised, according to the Anabaptist tradition, after the individual has achieved enough maturity to understand and consent of his or her own free will to the commitment of Amish life. Adult baptism for the Old Order then becomes an act that demands a total personal investment. Amish young people are usually baptised between the ages of fifteen and eighteen. Following the spring communion, they begin to take instruction that includes acquaintanceship with the rules and orders of the church as well as some Bible study. These sessions are held for approximately four months; then a date is set for the baptismal service, which is held before the second of the semiannual communion services in the fall. Baptism is performed by the bishop who pours water over the heads of the new members. The young people are given an opportunity to change their minds and are told that it is better not to take the vow than to do so and later break it.[10] Once the young person is baptised, he or she is admitted into full membership in the church, with all the subsequent privileges as well as responsibilities. However, in contrast to many religions that provide brief instruction to individuals planning to join the church, the Amish have in reality spent all the preceding years preparing the candidate for the special day. Church officials, parents, family members, peers, and other adults have all provided both precept and example in religious convictions and practices of the Old Order Amish.

The sacrament of the Lord's Supper is also an important part of the Old Order's religious activities. It is held twice a year in the spring and the fall; grape juice (or wine) and bread are served. The holding of a communion service is a sign that the community is unified and that no major rifts or divisions exist among the membership. The sacrament includes a "personal examination process" that begins two weeks before the communion. This service lasts for almost an entire day and all members must be present. The bishop and ministers state their views of the church rules, including any practices that might be forbidden in their community. Each member is then asked if he or she agrees with the rules and is in peace with the other members or if anything "stands in the way" of partaking of communion.[11] Two weeks later the communion service is held and also is an all-day affair. Following communion, foot washing takes place. The members divide into twos, with the sexes segregated, and wash each other's feet. This ritual is followed by the exchange of the "holy kiss" between the pair.[12] (See II Corinthians 13:12.) The foot washing reflects the true

humility of the members and also symbolizes the washing and
purification of the soul in the blood of Christ. (See John 13:4-17; I
Timothy 5:10.)

DEATH

The death of an Old Order Amish person is a solemn occasion
where the relatives grieve over the loss, but it usually does not involve
a sustained period of mourning. Death is taken as a matter of course.
Life has been lived to "store up treasures in heaven" rather than to
accumulate worldly goods, and death is looked upon as a natural part of
the life cycle and the time when one's reward is realized. There is,
however, much emphasis on remembering the person and his or her
role while living. Every issue of the *Budget* contains several "in
memoriams" to deceased Amish, mostly mothers or fathers. These
usually are poems that reflect the cherished role of the parents as well
as how greatly they have been missed by their family; many memorials
end with the same line, "Gone, but not forgotten." Typically, they
appear on the first or second anniversary of the death.

The burial process is usually carried out in the simplest way. Some
Amish communities have the bodies embalmed, but many do not. The
deceased is prepared for burial, the body washed and dressed by the
family and friends. The tasks of informing relatives; preparing the
burial site; constructing the plain, pine coffin; and other responsibilities
are carried out swiftly by relatives and neighbors. The immediate
family is relieved of all farming and domestic responsibilities as others
come in and take over these tasks. The chores are done on a minimal
basis for a short time. The close integrated nature of the Amish community is evident during a time of crisis such as death. In sharp contrast
to most non-Amish people who would think in terms of paying someone
for handling affairs at such a time, the Amish regard this as a part of
their responsibility to their brethren and payment is not considered.
This assistance then frees family members to greet mourners who come
to pay their respects. Often the body is kept in the home and someone
sits with the deceased on a twenty-four-hour basis; the funeral is
usually held on the third day following death. Each Amish community
has someone who makes coffins as they are needed.

Amish funerals are large affairs with relatives and friends coming
from long distances to attend. When a death occurs, it is common
practice to include in the *Budget* a list of out-of-town relatives and
friends attending the funeral; frequently this list is so long that it will
take up most of that particular column. If outside help is needed, such

as returning the deceased from a distant hospital, the local mortician will be asked to provide transportation. If the trip involves taking the body across a state line then embalming is required. The funeral sermon reflects the religious convictions of the Amish. The life of the deceased is not eulogized, nor are the individual's shortcomings emphasized. Instead the bishop or ministers discuss the fact that the Bible admonishes everyone to be ready to meet death. The young are reminded that death is inevitable, sometimes unexpected, and one should live so as to be prepared for that possibility. "The Lord giveth, and the Lord taketh away" is a strong theme at the time of death.

Every Amish community has a small cemetery. Usually a corner of some field is fenced off for that purpose. In most cemeteries family relationships are not recognized; individuals are buried in the order in which they die. The plots are kept to a minimal size, and in some communities a separate area is used for infants and children. No doubt this reflects frugality in land use since it is then possible to accommodate more burials. The headstone, made by someone in the community, is a small marker of concrete recording only the name of the deceased and dates of birth and death.

CONCLUSION

In the organization of church districts, the Old Order Amish have provided a system that allows for the optimum amount of interaction between members. The size of the church district allows each member to know the other members well. Yet, at the same time, it allows each district to determine worldly and nonworldly behavior, thus setting down both acceptable and nonacceptable practices for the church members. The positive result is that there is limited flexibility within Amish society; members who might appear to be violating rules in one community can move to another settlement and be accepted. Yet, overall, the Amish have not sacrificed the immeasurable strength and cohesion that stems from the small, individualized church district.

A subtle aspect of Amish society that often is not apparent, but is implied throughout their religious behavior, is their view that they are a chosen people. They do not flaunt the idea nor do they speak of it often. Their belief that they must be a humble people precludes any pronouncement that they regard themselves as special. Nevertheless, this is an extremely significant part of their overall religious philosophy and undoubtedly is another conviction that helps to bind them together.

Photo by Jan M. Skola

DRIVE-UP WINDOW,
FARMERS SAVINGS BANK,
KALONA.

Economic Organization

The Old Order Amish in Iowa live simply and take care of their own. These are perhaps the two significant characteristics that should be noted in describing their economic life-style and explaining their economic success. They reject most modern devices such as tractors and automobiles, believing that the old ways are more economical and less worldly. They maintain a high level of mutual assistance among their membership; no Amish is ever in want for monetary or physical assistance. The Amish practice extreme frugality in their spending habits, purchasing items only when absolutely necessary. Going hand in hand with their consumption austerity is their self-sufficiency in the areas of food and clothing. Amish women make most of the clothing for their families and most food needs are supplied through cultivation of large gardens and raising chickens and livestock. The Amish are an agricultural people, committed to the land both economically and religiously. Agrarian pursuits provide the foundation for their economic organization, which in turn makes possible most of their other economic practices.

THE PLAIN PEOPLE AND THE SOIL

A paramount consideration of the Amish is commitment to the soil, both in terms of its proper use as well as reliance upon it for their livelihood. The Amish believe that the only acceptable occupation is farming. One reason is, of course that they have never known any other environment, but more important they believe that as farmers they live closer to God and their rural way of life allows them to better serve Him. They consider themselves excellent farmers and feel a ''special kind of divine blessing'' is responsible for their success. Their religious convictions also affect their farming methods. If an Amishman farms in a way that causes the soil to lose its fertility, it is considered in some church districts to be as sinful as adultery or theft. The matter is then brought before the church membership, for they believe that ''he who robs the soil of its fertility sins against God and man.'' The Amish believe that each of them is a steward entrusted with the use of the soil. During their farming careers they must care for this resource in such a way that at retirement the land is in the same condition as when they took it over years before.[1]

Iowa's Old Order Amish carry on a diversified agricultural program. They follow a four-year crop rotation system, typically planting corn for two years, oats for one year, and a hay crop for the fourth year. They sell little if any of the grain raised but rather feed it to their livestock; frequently they need to purchase additional feed.

In keeping with the philosophy of stewardship, few Amish farmers use commercial fertilizer; instead they use large amounts of manure because they feel this is a superior method and a more natural one. A discussion with any Amish farmer about commercial additives such as fertilizers, insecticides, and pesticides will invariably bring a concerned response about the negative effects of these products. One Kalona Amishman pointed out that one year after treating a field for grasshoppers he thought perhaps the spraying had reduced the bird population around his farm. He started emphatically that he was not going to spray again and he also expressed fear that eventually the food produced on ground treated with many additives would be less nutritious and might carry residue from the chemicals, which would be detrimental to health. He pointed to a non-Amish neighbor who he said had raised corn for fifteen consecutive years on the same plot. The neighbor first applied manure, then tested the soil, and finally added the necessary amount of commercial fertilizer to bring the soil up to the desired level of fertility. The neighbor also made heavy use of insecticides. In the Amishman's opinion this farmer was only ''using the soil as a carrier''; he added that with all the fertilizers and other chemicals being used, ''he could just as well use an ashcan to raise corn.'' In regard to his own agricultural production, the Amishman declared that he felt satisfied with 100 bushels of corn to the acre because he knew he was maintaining soil fertility without adding any harmful substances.[2]

The Amish treatment of diseased livestock also frequently reflects their attitude of doing things the ''natural way.'' One Amish farmer, confronted with the problem of scours in his hogs, handled the problem in the following way. After first trying to save as many animals as he could, he then discontinued raising them in the hoghouse and instead turned his chickens loose in that building. He noted that the disease did not bother the chickens and that the "chicken bugs seemed to destroy the hog bugs." After about a year when he turned the chickens out and once again began to raise hogs in the hoghouse, the animals were no longer bothered with scours. Several other similar examples were recounted by Amish farmers, and in every case they made it clear that the process of switching over from one group of animals to another involved a thorough cleaning of the facility with all straw and refuse being burned. None, however, related using any chemical materials.[3]

MUTUAL ASSISTANCE

The Old Order Amish believe in private ownership of property, but this statement requires some explanation if their economic life is to be understood properly. They practice a high degree of mutual assistance that results in what could be termed a semicommunal society. It is one of the most significant advantages they enjoy in maintaining economic stability; at any time within any Amish community, every Amish family, although operating as a separate economic unit, has the backing of all members and potential use of all resources. Under certain circumstances they can also rely on assistance from Amish families living in other sections of the United States.

This practice of mutual aid extends to all areas of their lives but perhaps is most significant in regard to their financial needs. Because of their commitment to an agricultural way of life, they believe every married Amishman must have his own farm; this goal becomes the highest economic priority within the society. The young man may first work out as a hired hand and later as a tenant on another Amishman's farm, but these positions are regarded as temporary. When an Amishman marries, he is then given whatever help is necessary to become established as an independent farmer. He may continue to work as a tenant for a few years, but his final goal is land ownership. In many ways the total economic resources of the community are dedicated to this end. Sometimes the son or son-in-law receives his parents' farm as an outright gift; in other cases he can purchase it, but at a much lower price than if sold to a non-Amishman. In the event that his family or his wife's family is unable to help, he can depend on assistance from others in the community who have the financial means to help him. One Old Order Amishman in Kalona told of an interesting arrangement for arriving at an equitable price for the farmstead he was selling to his son-in-law. He himself first placed an evaluation on the land, the buildings, and the livestock but did not disclose these figures to his family. Then the son-in-law made up a separate list covering the same items, again without disclosing the amounts. An Amish neighbor was then called in to make up a third price list based on his separate evaluations. The Amish father-in-law then took the three sets of figures and averaged them. The resulting amounts were the prices paid by the son-in-law, and all parties were satisfied that an equitable arrangement had been made.[4]

When a young Amishman finds it necessary to borrow money to carry out the land transaction, family members will loan it at about half the interest rate, or less, than charged by a commercial firm. If money is borrowed from Amish families who are not relatives, the interest will be slightly higher but will still be substantially lower than the commercial rate.

With their ethic of self-help, the Amish discourage any investment outside the community, and excess earnings are retained for loans to young Amishmen. The Amish thus practice an atypical but highly advantageous financial system that encompasses the following features: (1) no money is borrowed unless necessary; (2) when money is borrowed, interest rates are low; (3) foreclosures are nonexistent; (4) bank failures and business failures only remotely affect them; and (5) interest and earnings remain within the community.[5] The economic security provided by this system does not preclude thoughtful, calm consideration over each transaction. The Amish are often slow to act in financial matters and do so only after a thorough assessment of the situation. A farmer in the Milton area, concerned that the price of land in that vicinity had gone above $200 an acre, stated that the Amish would wait it out and eventually the price would come back down. In the Kalona area an eighty-acre farm, located in the center of the Amish community, was sold at public auction. Many Amishmen were very interested in the land until it sold for $1,025 per acre.[6]

Mutual aid is highly beneficial in other financial areas as well. Amishmen do not believe in any commercial insurance but have an agreement among themselves that covers many different contingencies. For some losses, their insurance agreement calls for all Amish families to share expenses when the damage exceeds $60. In the event that a church member losses a farm building due to fire or windstorm, the farmer suffering the misfortune will pay one-fourth the cost himself and the remaining three-fourths is divided among others in the group. The loss is appraised by three church members, and reimbursement takes place on that basis. Settlement is usually reached within sixty days. The share of each individual family is determined by an Amish church representative who goes to the county courthouse and checks the evaluation of all the members' property—personal and real estate; each family is then assessed a specific amount based on ability to pay. Mutual aid funds are also collected at communion services when, toward the end, the bishop talks about charity and asks each member to make a contribution. The money is kept in a fund and used when necessary. To spread the financial burden among more families, the larger Iowa Old Order communities are aligned with church districts outside the state. Buchanan County members have joined with church districts in Wisconsin to form an insurance group, while the Kalona, Milton, and Jamesport, Missouri, Old Order Amish constitute a second insurance district.[7]

When an Amishman finds it necessary to borrow from someone outside his community, usually the local bank, the loan is partially underwritten by his church district. Church members draw up a document in which they agree to reimburse the Amishman if he loses any buildings through fire or windstorm. Since the bank holds a mortgage on the Amishman's property, however, the church district promises instead to pay the money for the losses to the bank. This agreement is then signed by the person requesting the loan and the bishop of his church district. (A sample of such an agreement is given in Appendix B.) In recent years the Iowa Amish have found it necessary to borrow from sources outside their own communities. A Kalona banker has stated that they usually do not borrow as much as non-Amish farmers, and the debt is usually for a shorter time. He expressed the highest regard for the Amish as customers and said that he never hesitates to loan them money. The banker added that in some instances he does not require any signed paper from them.[8]

If Amish families are unable to pay their medical bills or other expenses, these are paid by the entire church district. The matter is handled by the bishop, who collects the bills, assesses each family in the district according to their ability to pay, and then reimburses the creditor. The Amish enjoy impeccable reputations of honesty with all local merchants. One retailer in Buchanan County who has a large Amish trade stated that in twenty-three years of doing business with them, he had only one Amishman who did not pay his bill. The bill was paid, however, when within a short time the man's bishop heard of the difficulty, came to the merchant inquiring about the amount of the bill, and returned in a few days with the money.[9]

The Amish are aware of one another's needs because most families subscribe to the newspaper, the *Budget*. Published weekly at Sugar Creek, Ohio, by a non-Amish newspaperman, the paper carries news accounts from most Amish settlements in North and South America as well as from conservative Mennonite communities. Families eagerly look forward to the arrival of the *Budget,* and any delay in delivery invariably results in a comment by the *Budget* reporter in the following week's column. In their reporting local scribes include details of births, marriages, deaths, and any accidents or other unusual happenings. All farm sales are listed as well as any moves into or out of the Amish communities. The reporters also include considerable information on health matters. If a person has been ill for any length of time, a weekly progress report is usually included. Accounts dealing with illness, accidents, and death bring forth letters of concern and often monetary help for the unfortunate family from other Amish all over the United States. Sometimes the contributors know the other party personally, but many times they do not. These contributions have been known to add up to thousands of dollars. One Amish family in the Milton community received almost $300 when their newborn child died.[10]

Two other significant areas of mutual assistance are building construction and agricultural cooperation. The Amish frequently purchase old buildings, which they then either move to their own farms or tear down to retrieve the lumber. These tasks are shared among many neighbors. When a farmer finds it necessary to build a new barn or house, he calls on his neighbors to assist him. The event is termed a ''frolic'' and is well publicized throughout the community. On the day appointed for the construction to take place, the Amishman holding the frolic has all the necessary tools and materials assembled. If a foundation is necessary, this has been constructed. The neighbors arrive early in the morning, and the entire day is spent in hard work. The Amish wife, often with the help of relatives or friends, prepares the noon meal. Farmers also cooperate by forming threshing rings; here several men, usually five, band together to purchase a thresher and then at harvest time rotate from one member's farm to another, pooling their labor as well as their capital. This results in considerable savings in both machinery investment and labor costs. The trend, however, has been for fewer farmers to be involved in this practice as well as a smaller number of families in each threshing ring.

As well as being apparent in explicit ways, the Amish commitment to mutual aid is an implicit concern that permeates their daily lives. The difficulties of one family—whether moral, social, or economic—are of deep concern to every other family. In the Milton community, one family appeared to be in financial difficulty, and it was feared that they would not be able to keep up the payments on their farm. This was a matter of great concern for all Amish families in that area regardless of whether there would be a specific request for financial assistance.

IDEAL OF AUSTERITY

Another highly significant aspect of the economic practices of the Iowa Old Order Amish is their attitude toward expenditures. The Amish embrace the "ideal of austerity" in their buying habits. Put in the simplest terms, this means that they spend very little money.[11] The Amish carefully weigh every expenditure and then buy only necessities. Their religious beliefs prohibit spending on jewelry, nonbiblical books, commercial entertainment, cosmetics, and haircuts; entertainment devices like television sets and radios are also rejected. Of more significance is the belief that electricity, telephones, and automobiles are too worldly and should therefore be banned. The ban on electricity alone rules out high-priced home devices like central heating and appliances such as automatic washing machines and dryers. In an Amish home one usually finds a gasoline-powered washing machine, a small oil or kerosene space heater in the main rooms of the house, and of course, the buggies housed in the shed. Not only does the Amish farmer save on initial investments for automobiles and appliances but his simpler devices require almost no upkeep expenditures. In most homes there are no rugs on the floor, no upholstered sofas or chairs, and no curtains at the windows. Thus few items will wear out and need replacement or will require upkeep.

The Amish are particularly frugal about the purchase of farm machinery and weigh these expenditures very carefully; unless there is an absolute need for a new or different implement, it is not purchased. In the Kalona area, the average amount invested in machinery per Old Order Amish farm has been estimated at approximately $1,500.[12] Most machinery is about forty or fifty years old but will continue to be used as long as it can be repaired. Amishmen are highly adept at fashioning replacement parts, since in many instances new ones are no longer available. Most use horses for fieldwork, so equipment needs are simplified and the life of the equipment indefinitely prolonged. When questioned about replacement parts, they reply that if their equipment is kept well oiled and in good repair, new parts are seldom needed. When they do need to purchase an additional piece of farm machinery they will scour the countryside for used equipment and will make a

THRESHING TIME.

Photo by Joan Liffring Zug

purchase only after a thorough search has been made. Invariably the item purchased will be used rather than new. The Amish are great shoppers, attending farm sales, auctions, and horse sales throughout Iowa. Many times they travel to communities in neighboring states to attend farm and horse sales.[13]

The Amish frequently joke among themselves about their austere spending habits as well as their ability to make and save money. In the Kalona area, the Amish tell about one of their more well-to-do members who made a trip to Oregon. While there, he visited a lumber mill and decided to buy a boxcarload of lumber and have it shipped back to his farm in Iowa. Officials from the lumber firm called a Kalona banker to inquire about the man's financial status. They were advised that not only did the Amishman have the means to purchase a boxcarload of lumber but with his wealth the lumber firm should try to sell him an entire trainload![14]

The Amish settlements differ slightly in their use of farm equipment; the Kalona Amish use tractors for fieldwork, while the other communities do not. When tractors first came on the market, the

machines were expensive as well as being cumbersome and difficult to maneuver in small fields. The Amish believed that the machines packed the ground and contributed to poor farming methods because they did not get into the corners of the fields and left land untouched along the fences. Since they were expensive and also contributed to careless farming methods, their use could not be justified. Other Amish have rejected the tractor purely for traditional reasons. One farmer explained that use of tractors for fieldwork would reduce the reliance on horses and very possibly lead to their replacement by automobiles for travel purposes. Since opposition to automobiles is very strong, they hope to avoid such a transition by heavy reliance on horsepower. Where tractors are used, however, they must be equipped with steel wheels.[15]

Not all Kalona Amish take advantage of the rules, however, since some farmers feel that tractors, like other modern machinery, have a negative influence on their sons. One farmer stated that he had owned a tractor for ten years but that several years ago he had decided to sell it because of the high cost of fuel and upkeep; he returned to the use of horses and stated that this method was cheaper. He also believed the tractor had a bad influence on his sons because they would not learn to farm without one. If they were accustomed to farming with horses, they could have more flexibility and would then have a choice between the two methods. Raised with tractors, however, they would lack the other experience.[16]

AMISH INGENUITY

Even without modern agricultural equipment and energy sources such as electricity, many Amishmen are highly skilled in utilizing the resources available to them. To lighten their work load and make their lives a little more comfortable, many farmers use gasoline or diesel engines to power machines that would otherwise require hand labor. One Old Order Amishman, while residing in Buchanan County, had constructed a series of devices on his farm that vividly demonstrated his ingenuity in both simplifying some of his operations as well as lightening his work load. As a part of his farming operation he raised pigs and stressed a regular schedule of farrowing, one that continued throughout the entire year. Acquiring a used, hand-fired boiler, the farmer had constructed a farrowing operation that not only minimized his labor but also assured a higher rate of survival for the young pigs. In the farrowing building, he had built several pens, each with a separate concrete slab between twelve to fifteen feet in length. He had poured the slabs fairly thick and somewhat slanted and had embedded water pipes which were connected to the hot water side of the boiler. There was a difference of several inches in height between the entry and the exit levels of the pipes.[17]

The Amishman had utilized his knowledge of air and water convection in the operation of the system. No pump was connected to the pipes, but a system of valves was incorporated so that all air could be exhausted from the lines. As the water heated in the boiler, a natural convection was established so that the water flowed through the slabs without the benefit of a pump. The farmer commented that natural convection was quite slow and that the slabs did not heat up uniformly, but he had taken that factor into account during the planning stage and had turned it into an advantage. By opening and closing the valves connected with each slab, the amount of hot water flowing through could be controlled. The result was that they became much warmer on the entry end of the system than on the exit end. The farmer noted that he could walk with bare feet over the whole slab; but if he stood at the hot end, it eventually became uncomfortable, although he could remain standing indefinitely on the cooler end. He pointed out that when the pigs were first born, the sow remained at the heated end of the slab, moving gradually toward the cooler end as the brood became stronger. The movement of the sow depended upon the time of year and the outside temperature; during very cold weather the sow used the warmer end of the slab for a much longer time. As soon as the animals remained at the cool end of the slab, the farmer knew that they would not suffer from exposure and could be safely turned out of the pen.[18]

On the same farm, the dairy barn offered another example of resourcefulness. Hanging in the building were the usual number of pails and utensils necessary for a milking operation, but in one corner a bucket with numerous holes in the bottom was suspended. The Amish-man explained that the bucket was not worthless but, quite the contrary, he had placed it there for a specific reason. He then pointed out a small diesel engine that was used to pump water for the farm. The cord suspending the pail was also attached to a lever on the engine. When the water supply ran low, the farmer started the pump by hand and then placed the shut-off lever in a certain position. The pump first filled the reservoir; when the tank was completely filled, the excess water escaped through an overflow pipe into the milk house. The bucket with the holes was placed beneath the overflow pipe so that after the tank was full, water ran into the bucket. As the bucket filled and dropped, it pulled the lever by the pump, thus turning off the engine. By then the purpose of the bucket was rather obvious but still unexplained were the holes in the bottom. With a delightful grin, our Amish friend related that he had calculated the flow of water from the overflow pipe into the bucket and then carefully made the holes so that the water drained out more slowly than it flowed in. This provided two benefits: first, he did not have to make a trip to the milk house to turn off the switch each time he used it, and, second, the water drained out of the bucket so that in cold weather it did not freeze, thus disrupting the procedure.[19]

This enterprising young farmer had also used the water supply in another unusual way to provide a cooling system for the storage of food in his house. Checking the temperature of the water as it was pumped from the ground, he discovered it was in the mid-fifties and remained constant throughout the year. He then laid a pipe from the pump into the house and circulated the cool water throughout a small insulated room; another pipe then returned the water to the barn. In this manner he had developed a summer storage place for fruits and vegetables which, while not refrigerated in the strictest sense, nevertheless was many degrees cooler than other rooms in the house.[20]

ECONOMIC SELF-SUFFICIENCY

The cash income of the Amish is derived from a number of sources. Most farmers carry on a regular pig farrowing program, and this provides an almost continual source of income throughout the year. Many maintain small dairy herds and the milk sold represents a major portion of the farm income. Extra horses may be sold, although occasionally farmers find it necessary to purchase an additional horse or two.

The Amish strive to raise as much food as possible through their gardening and livestock programs. Every family has a large garden, sometimes covering three-fourths of an acre, in which they raise a multitude of vegetables. The women can large quantities of vegetables, and in late summer, at the lowest market price, they also preserve large quantities of peaches and other fruits. In many homes, canning is a family affair with everyone helping out. The process is set up so each member has a different responsibility, and the whole process resembles an assembly line. One family reported canning almost 2,000 quarts of food in one summer. The families' meat supply is filled through home production; the Amish raise and slaughter a few pigs and cows each year in addition to their regular livestock program. Every farmstead includes chickens and sometimes turkeys and a few geese.[21]

Some Amish families now own bottled gas freezers, and this method of food preservation has partially replaced canning. Other families rent space at their local community frozen food locker and preserve much of their food in that manner. With such home food production, families need to buy only staple items like sugar and flour. The following story illustrates the near self-sufficiency the Amish have achieved in their food requirements. In recent years the Kalona business community has arranged a limited number of tours for outsiders to visit Amish homes in that area. One tour included a total of forty-four women from out of state, and local officials thought it would be interesting for the visitors if they could eat at noon in an Amish home. One was selected and a full-course meal was served by the Amish hostess and her daughters. Asked later if the preparations had been too strenuous, the mother replied that it had not been bad and in fact, she "didn't have to go to town for a single thing."[22]

THE HITCHING RACK.

Courtesy of the **Des Moines Register and Tribune**

In the area of clothing needs, Amish wives and daughters make most of the garments needed by their families. With the unchanging styles an article of clothing is never discarded but handed down from one family member to the next and worn until it is literally falling apart. This practice significantly reduces expenditures, particularly in view of the large number of children.

Activities such as these have helped the Amish maintain their strong, productive family units, with a sense of togetherness, and hence they have not suffered disintegration from loss of function as have so many other non-Amish American families. Their self-sufficiency is made posssible in part by their large families, as the Amish have birthrates among the highest in the world. Families of seven to nine children are typical. A visit to an Amish farm at any time of year leaves little doubt that all family members who are able have work assignments. There is an implicit awareness on the part of Amish youngsters that hard work is not only a necessity but also a challenge to be accepted cheerfully, and in the process it becomes something of a blessing. The sight of an Amish child, barely old enough to toddle, insisting on imitating her mother by helping to set the table or two preschoolers determined to help their father by carrying a pail of feed so heavy that to keep it from dragging on the ground, they must hold the handle above their heads, vividly underscores the Amish attitude toward work and the resulting practices. Children begin to help their parents at an early age and are given limited responsibility by the time they are six. The Amish believe deeply that they must teach their children to work hard and accept responsibility. Because of their large families, the Amish are able to reject laborsaving devices, relying instead on hand labor; moreover, few if any Amish farmers need to hire outside help.

OUTSIDE EMPLOYMENT

Old Order Amish families allow their young people to seek outside employment for a limited period. This practice appears in all three major Iowa Amish communities, although it is most widespread in Kalona. Many teenagers work outside the home from the time they finish grade school until they marry. This is accepted as a way of supplementing the family income but is regarded as temporary. In Kalona, Amish girls work as salespeople, bakery clerks, and cleaning women; the men work primarily as carpenters. Wages are turned over to the families, a practice that is followed until the age of twenty-one. If teenagers work at home, they are not paid until they are twenty-one;

when they reach that age, however, their parents pay them or they seek outside employment. Parents expect that when the young people marry, they will settle on farms.

Parents also sometimes supplement their income with outside work. In all three major Old Order Iowa communities men do carpentry work, lay cinder blocks, and move houses. Women sell eggs throughout the year, and in the summertime they sell garden produce like tomatoes and sweet corn. Sometimes these products are sold door to door, but most sales are made from the home. In each of the Amish communities at least one woman bakes bread, cookies, sweet rolls, and pies for sale to the general public. In some homes a special room is set aside for the baking and display of goods. Usually a small, hand-painted sign with the words "bread" or "baked goods" is placed alongside the road to advertise the items. Both parents and offspring have widespread reputations as being "very hard workers." Rarely do employers or neighbors of the Amish fail to point out this characteristic of the Plain People. Many non-Amish farmers who have hired young Amishmen as farm workers have commented that they "know how to go ahead on their own and do not always have to be told what to do."

In a few cases Amishmen pursue occupations other than farming, but they are always farm related. In both Kalona and Buchanan County men maintain harness and leather shops that supply their brethren with leather goods and provide a repair service. In Kalona the harness shop also repairs buggies. An Amishman may handle the dealership for farm equipment frequently used by other members. Both communities have small stores operating from farm homes, offering yard goods, shoes, hats, dishes, and other articles that Amish families buy on a regular basis. In Buchanan County an Amishman who has retired from farming pursues cabinet and furniture making in his home.

LIMITED LANDHOLDINGS

One of the characteristics of Old Order Amish society becoming increasingly evident in the Midwest is the size of individual land holdings. As their non-Amish neighbors continually increase farm size, the Amish maintain their traditional holdings of around 100 acres and in so doing are placed in sharper and sharper contrast with them. The Amish have farmed this much acreage for almost 100 years and have very strong convictions as to the desirability of continuing this pattern. Any conversation with an Amish farmer will sooner or later get around to the topic of farm size, and he will inevitably state his strong opposition to any of his brethren enlarging their holdings or buying more than one farm. Their reasoning is simple: if families begin to buy more than one farm, there will not be enough land to go around. One constant reason given for forbidding rubber tires on buggies or farm equipment is that it would make it too easy to get from one field to another, hence making it possible for one Amishman to operate more than one farm. The Amish believe that development of a tenant class would be a second negative consequence. Amish owners would hire nonowners to work the farms, thus some families would be deprived of being independent. Throughout Amish communities, then, societal attitudes are strongly set against larger land ownership patterns that would usurp available land, create an inequality among members, and perhaps lead to a tenant class.[23]

Although the Amish have a telling point in their rationale, there is a much broader consideration involved as well. While some have acquired great wealth through expert management, the majority of Amish farmers face a limited level of profit because of small farm size. When the Old Order Amish are compared to other American utopian groups, the Amish appear to have solved one very bothersome problem that plagued many during their final years. In the history of the Icarians, the Amanas, and the Shakers, to mention just a few of the more prominent utopian groups, a common characteristic evident at the time of their demise was economic affluence. Typically, these societies started out with limited resources and through concerted group effort managed to pay off mortgages, expand holdings, and develop profitable commerce with the outside world. The growing wealth within the society meant that later generations did not have to work as hard (a fact of which they were cognizant) as their parents and grandparents. As affluence developed in each group, there was a corresponding loss of the zeal, cohesion, and idealism that had been highly evident in the first generation. In South Dakota the Hutterites, regarded as one of the most successful utopian groups of all time, are experiencing a similar problem with their young people. In at least one colony the Hutterite elders have been forced to give each young person a limited amount of monthly spending money. Since the early 1500s the Hutterites have been a communal society in which there were no private possessions nor individual dispersement of funds. The present generation are aware, however, of their society's wealth, and because of this condition they realize that they do not have to work as hard nor be as saving as their fathers and grandfathers before them.[24]

The Old Order Amish, with their strong sentiment against increased farm size, appear for the most part to have avoided the problem of increasing group affluence and individual wealth. Given their limited land and property holdings, most of the present generation of Amish farmers have no more financial resources than their fathers or grand-fathers.

CONCLUSION

The great, all encompassing feature of Old Order Amish economic life is their belief in the superiority of agrarian living. Their religion demands that they work as farmers, and this foundation makes most of their economic practices possible as well as reinforcing religious and social beliefs. A rural environment provides separation from the outside world and a high degree of economic self-sufficiency. In a rural setting with a minimum of expenditures, large families produce an abundant labor supply and are therefore assets rather than liabilities. The simple manner of living allows tight restriction of all expenditures. The Amish policy of mutual assistance provides a pooling of community resources that results in greater strength and solidarity. Without the agricultural setting it is doubtful if the Old Order Amish could survive.

WINTERTIME FUN.

Courtesy of the Des Moines Register and Tribune

C H A P T E R   F I V E

In all cultures family structure is significant, but to the Old Order Amish it is crucial because in their society the family controls the entire range of life activities. Socialization of the young is almost totally controlled by parents because of their belief that Amish people should be separated from the world. Within that sphere, most parents provide formal education for their offspring through the maintenance of parochial schools. Religious training begins when the child is very young and continues throughout the formative years until the time of baptism; it is all-pervading because daily religious services are held in the home, religious education is included in the school curriculum, and the major social activities of the young take place in a religious setting. When the Amish child finishes the eighth grade, the parents provide an intensive vocational training period where the emphasis is on "learning by doing." Even when Amish members reach retirement age, they are cared for within the home rather than being placed in a retirement home or care center.

Family Life

    An Old Order Amish farmstead fairly hums with activity every day of the week except Sunday. The Amish are early risers, and on a typical workday after a hearty breakfast, everyone is ready to go to work. Frequently the Amish father will use the breakfast hour to discuss the day's work with his older sons. The mother may also use this time to tell her daughters about the work schedule. Even without instructions, however, each knows from experience what his or her responsibilities will be.

    During every season, the men have different tasks to accomplish. Any comment to them concerning the work load invariably brings a response that they are working hard because they want to, not because they are compelled to. During the winter months there is always some "fixing up" to do around the farm, machinery to repair, or perhaps some building that needs to be done. With horses and a small dairy herd, the job of providing feed is continual. If their own work is light, they will perhaps help a relative or maybe give the bishop a

55

helping hand. If a horse or farm sale is being held in the vicinity, the Amish father and older sons will probably attend, hoping to find a bargain or two.

Inside the house the scene is much the same. By midmorning of any weekday the mother and her older daughters have many different jobs under way. The sewing machine may be whirring as a teenager stitches up a new dress for herself or helps out with the mending; a pot is boiling away on the stove as the noon meal is prepared; on the kitchen cupboard a batch of bread is rising, soon to be punched down and placed into pans for baking. Like her husband, the Amish wife follows a seasonal work schedule, which means that there is much to do every day. With her large family, she faces a heavy work load in completing the minimum necessities such as preparing three meals a day; washing, ironing, and mending the family's clothing; and cleaning the house. Along with these responsibilities, however, the women must also complete special work at different times of the year. During the spring a large garden is planted. During the summer months the garden requires constant care, and in late summer the produce must be canned. Summer is also the time when Amish women must sew the children's school clothing as well as that for other family members. No doubt there are also other outside projects to be done during the summer months such as painting buildings or yard work.

The relationship between most family members is close. The family size leaves little room or time for privacy or isolation from other members. Rather, it appears that the children have learned to depend on one another for companionship as well as for assistance with their work. Outward signs of affection may be uncommon, but a pervading sense of concern for one another can be felt through the entire household. A warm bond of affection appears to exist between family members and they obviously enjoy one another. As in any home, affection is often expressed in a humorous way, with family members teasing one another and joking about each other's activities. One topic that will always produce some reaction in any Amish home is the matter of courting. One Amish father was amused with his daughter because of her constant concern over receiving a letter from her boyfriend who lived in another state. The father laughingly told his daughter that because she was always standing by the side of the road waiting for the mailman with her hand outstretched, he thought he would take down the mailbox because they simply did not need it any more. [1]

The relations between husband and wife are determined to a large extent by the strong patriarchal nature of Amish society. The father is head of the household and is the family spokesman in all matters, both within the Amish community as well as outside. Wives are somewhat retiring, at least with non-Amish, and play a less significant role in determining family relations. Nevertheless, at times all the family come together to discuss matters that affect each member, and in these cases they frequently reach joint decisions. When decisions are stated to outsiders they are rarely phrased, "My wife and I decided to move," but rather in terms such as "My wife wanted to get near her folks, and I decided that it was a good time to move."

The Amish believe in the biblical injunction that man was created in "the image and glory of God" but woman was made for "the glory of the man."[2] (See I Corinthians 11:7.) They regard marriage as a natural relationship between men and women and assume that all but a few of their people will marry. Those who do not frequently have some physical or mental impairment. When death occurs, the widow or widower frequently remarries within a respectable time. Within the family the husband and wife maintain a close relationship. Displays of affection may be rare, but the Amish believe that a person's commitment to his or her spouse is second only to commitment to God.[3]

The home itself is frequently a combination of the old and the new. Amish houses are roomy, with large kitchens, dining rooms, living rooms, and many bedrooms. The walls of the main rooms are usually painted a pastel shade of blue, green, or yellow, and few pictures or decorations are placed on them. Sometimes the family will hang a picture of their farmstead, or sometimes a calendar, but no pictures of people. The living room and dining room furniture is plain and solid and has probably been in use for many years. There may be several rocking chairs in the living room, a library table or a desk, and a sofa that is frequently on the order of a deacon's bench. If the piece is upholstered, usually the arms and legs are wooden so it will be plainer and also wear longer. Most Amish homes do not have curtains at the windows but have roll-up shades that can be pulled down at night for privacy. All floors are typically hardwood and left uncovered in every room but the kitchen and bathroom where linoleum or similar floor covering is used. A few handmade braided rugs may be scattered around, but for the most part the floors are plain. Most Amish homes do not contain coat closets; instead, hooks are placed near the main door for coats and other wearing apparel. If there are small children in the household, toys are usually kept in one corner of either the dining room or living room. The children have coloring books, toy cars and trucks, building blocks, dolls, doll furniture and clothing, wooden barnyard animals, miniature barns, and a limited number of games.

The one feature that never varies from one Amish home to another

THE PARLOR.

is the hook located in the ceiling of each room. At dusk the housewife lights a kerosene lantern and hangs it on the hook. Another constant feature is the oil burner or coal stove in the corner of the dining room or living room. If the unit is small, there is one in both rooms.

The furnishings in Amish kitchens vary widely depending on the community. In Kalona, many homes are quite new or have been remodeled and contain beautiful modern kitchens, complete with built-in wooden cabinets, hot and cold running water, modern sink and sewage system, and modern bottled gas refrigerators and ranges. On the other hand, because they cannot use electricity, they do not have electric washing machines, clothes dryers, garbage disposals, or dish-washers. In all cases, however, the kitchens are large enough to accommodate many working at one time. Many Kalona Amish families also have bathrooms. On the other hand, most Buchanan County Amish households have wood-burning kitchen ranges, ice boxes, and outside toilets.

The washing facilities also vary; sometimes these are located in the basement, sometimes in a back room or in a shed located a short distance from the house. On washday, the Amish housewife generally

AN OLD ORDER
AMISH KITCHEN.

THE PUMP.

uses a washing machine powered by a gasoline engine. The Maytag Company continues to manufacture a gasoline-powered model with a top wringer that is advertised regularly in the *Budget.*

Mealtime is an important part of the day because all family members come together then. There is a serious time for prayer, but there may also be joking and general good humor. The father sits at the head of the table, with the mother to his left. Each family member has a place at the table. The boys sit, ranging in age from the oldest to the youngest, to the father's right; the girls sit on their mother's side, in the same order. The baby is placed next to the mother to be fed.[4] When the food is ready, all the serving dishes are placed on the table, including the dessert, and everyone is seated. The older girls bring refills from the kitchen when necessary, and usually the mother remains seated during the entire meal.

The Amish eat well. The dishes they serve are basic, but food is plentiful. The women are generally considered to be excellent cooks by the Amish themselves as well as outsiders. A typical noon meal, the main one of the day, would include meat, potatoes, gravy, a fresh or home-canned vegetable, homemade bread, pickles, jelly, posssibly a gelatin dish, fresh fruit in season, and possibly cake or pie for dessert. Milk is served at every meal, but coffee and tea are not served in all Amish households. Two particular food favorites of Amish families are tomato gravy, served over bread for breakfast, and banana soup. Amish women do a great deal of baking and their families constantly enjoy pastries and homemade bread and rolls. Since they raise large gardens, a wide variety of vegetables is available to serve throughout the year. They also raise strawberries, rhubarb, and melons as well as growing raspberry bushes and apple and cherry trees. Because they raise their own livestock, the meat supply is also ample and varied. In all Amish communities, families rent space at the local frozen food locker plant so they can freeze at least part of their meat supply rather than relying completely on canning or salting.

CHILDREN

The average Amish couple will have seven to nine children. Large families are an economic asset, but beyond that the Amish have a religious commitment to this practice. They interpret the biblical passage "go forth and multiply" in a literal way. If a couple remains childless after a year or so of marriage, other Amish members begin to wonder why.

Another aspect of religious motivation related to family size is their rejection of proselytism. Many religious groups rely heavily on conversion of outsiders to increase their church membership rolls. Since the Old Order do not follow this procedure, they must rely strictly on their own members for continuation and increase of population. Frequently when a couple who has only one or two children is asked about their family size, they will respond with "we were only able to have two," implying that they would have had a larger family if possible. When talking about specific families, church leaders will make similar comments such as "they were only able to have two children" or "they had three children but they lost one." The comments indicate that church officials are aware of the child-bearing status of families in their church district.[5]

Children begin to assist their parents at an early age, thus an Amish farmstead operates as an economic system that includes the children's labor. A few activities may be aesthetic in nature, such as working in the flower garden, but most tasks are significant and the children know they are an integral part of the economic makeup of the family. Both children and young adults are involved in day-to-day activities that encourage familial rather than individual accomplishment. This situation is further reenforced by the fact that no Amish child is paid for work until the age of twenty-one.[6]

One aspect of child rearing never overlooked in an Amish home is the matter of discipline; parents are loving, but firm. They believe they are charged with the responsibility of rearing their children to love and honor God, to embrace and perpetuate the Amish way of life, and to learn how to accept responsibility and hard work. They believe firmly that if they spare the child and fail to punish for wrongdoing, the child will suffer. The parents present a united front so the child will realize there can be no playing on the sympathy of either without the other knowing about it. Physical punishment is used frequently, not in bitterness or anger, but with the firm conviction that it is for the child's own good; the children realize that certain actions on their part will undoubtedly result in a whipping or some other form of punishment. The following excerpt from the writings of Menno Simons vividly reflects the Amish attitude toward child rearing:

Instruct your children
from youth up
and daily admonish them with the word of the Lord
setting a good example.

Teach
and admonish them
to the extent of their understanding.

Constrain and punish them with discretion
and moderation
without anger or bitterness
lest they be discouraged.

Do not spare the rod if necessity requires it
He that is too lenient with his child
Is frightened whenever he hears a cry.

A child unrestrained becomes headstrong as
an untamed horse.
Give him no liberty in his youth
and wink not at his follies.
Bow down his neck while he is young
Lest he wax stubborn and be disobedient to thee.

Correct they son
and keep him from idleness
lest thou be ashamed
On his account.[7]

SEX ROLE LEARNING AND IDENTIFICATION

While most non-Amish families encounter continual difficulty in
the selection of vocations for their offspring, the Amish experience
none of these frustrations. Because they believe that agriculture is the
only acceptable occupation, the young men need vocational training in
that area and the young girls need assistance in learning the domestic
tasks of a farm wife. Unlike non-Amish young people who face a
constantly changing society because of technological and scientific
advances, Amish young people learn the same skills their grandparents
and great-grandparents learned before them. Thus for the Amish child
this narrow range of activities means that sex role learning and identification change very little from generation to generation. The child
learns, not so much from contemplation, but from precept and example.

Young girls are early introduced to and constantly involved with
domestic responsibility. Daughters are taught by their mothers to cook

Amish food, sew Amish clothing, can large quantities of food, and undertake all other traditionally expected tasks. Because of constant interaction with other Amish girls, it is known that they too are learning the same responsibilities. Given the large family sizes, most daughters, regardless of their position in the family, learn the techniques of child rearing from experience. For the youngest daughter who has no little brother or sister to care for, there is the opportunity to "hire out" to other Amish families who need additional domestic help. In fact, this practice is so common that when a woman has a baby, not only is that information included in the *Budget,* but invariably the name of the hired girl is also given. Because of these practices, Amish girls have been completely trained in what their society views as traditional work areas before they marry and begin to repeat the life cycle.

The Amish male experiences a similar process. He too is socialized by the family, most particularly the father. By accompanying and assisting his father in the fields, the young man learns what he needs to know about the soil and the planting of crops. He learns about the proper use and care of farm machinery as well as the care of livestock. In the Kalona area, Amish farmers are recognized for their ability to breed and successfully raise large numbers of swine.[8] By watching his father, the boy learns that baby pigs need a great deal of attention if early signs of disease or illness are to be quickly detected. The same process is repeated over and over with other agricultural tasks. In observing his father in community functions, the son develops the understanding that when he reaches adulthood, he will as the head of the household give freely and cheerfully of his time to his fellow Amishmen, his church, and his school.

An additional consideration of the similar upbringing that all the young people receive is what might be called "interchangeability." When a boy or girl reaches the age of sixteen, which marks the beginning of courtship, they know that any member of the opposite sex has the same life-style as themselves. Every Amish boy knows that any Amish girl he desires to court will know how to cook, sew, and care for children and that she shares his religious beliefs. Certainly there are many individual differences, but overall they share a common heritage and upbringing that binds them together in a homogeneous life-style. At marriage young people know they are making a commitment for the remainder of their lives or until their spouse dies because the Amish do not accept divorce among their members. As one Amish bishop put it, "Amish marry with the intention of staying married." The same bishop then added that couples considering marriage must make certain they are compatible and not just merely infatuated with each other or suffering from a case of puppy love. He stated that couples should not marry until they are certain about their true feelings because "Puppy love leads to a dog's life."[9] The concept of interchangeability is very significant in understanding the high level of stability in Amish society.

ADULTHOOD

The Anabaptist heritage of the Old Order dictates that baptism will take place when a person reaches adulthood. Within Amish society this conviction of adult baptism provides a phenomenon that may be interpreted as a "rite of passage." For the young person reared in this faith being baptized, and therefore becoming a full-fledged member of the church, is an individual decision and one that is taken after very serious thought. The decision is usually made at about fifteen to eighteen years of age. By this time the young person understands fully the implications of the decision. The life-long process of socialization and the negative comparisons with outside society as an alternative now demand a binding decision from each individual since the choice of the Amish way determines a permanent life-style.

At times, however, this stage does not arrive without rebellion on the part of some, particularly the Amish boys. The number involved is no more than 10 percent of the young adults, a very small amount of the total age group. These young men race their horses, often purchase forbidden items like transistor radios, drive automobiles, and attend movies. Sometimes the transgressions become more severe, like drinking alcohol. There has been, however, no evidence of experimenting with drugs. On a few occasions, get-togethers of the young people have turned into rowdy affairs that required adult intervention. Some parents expect and tolerate a certain amount of resistance and rule breaking, and if not too severe they simply close their eyes to it. Many others, however, believe it is wrong to bend the rules even a little, and these parents refuse to accept any deviant behavior without serious reprisals. However, like their non-Amish neighbors, most adults view this as a time of transition that their children will soon outgrow. Non-Amish parents often take the position that as soon as their children marry and settle down, things will work out all right. For the Amish, the end of the rebellious stage is marked by baptism and membership in the church.[10]

One important contrast, however, between non-Amish and Amish young people is the age at which the rebellion period ends. Non-Amish children are exposed to influences outside their home at a very early age. Once in school, usually at age five, the children have wide contact with other life-styles through their peer groups. In addition, most non-Amish young people marry and become parents at a later age, and thus experience the "settling down" period later (usually in the early or mid-twenties) than the Old Order. In contrast, the Old Order youngster is much less influenced by the outside world during early development, has a shorter period in which active rebellion can take place, and makes a commitment for a future life-style at a younger age. The Amish will not allow young people to marry until they have been baptized. It is significant that all factors minimize the time for youthful resistance to Old Order ways before the young seek definite commitment toward the Amish life. Yet this decision comes late enough so that it is made by the individual who is to assume the adult status. Occasionally Amish young people complain about the restrictive nature of their lives and express a desire to go to town more often or perhaps have less work to do around the farm. However, once they have made their decision and have been baptized into the Amish faith, complaints are rarely heard. The system operates, therefore, to accommodate some resistance and criticism but to keep this period as short as possible while still maintaining the decision of baptism as one of individual choice.

The Amish mother and father face heavy and exhausting tasks in the early years of their marriage, but as the children become more capable of assuming responsibility the parental roles change significantly. Since farm size does not increase as the family members grow older, the parents are able to be less involved in the actual physical work and adopt greater roles as supervisors. Decision making in almost all matters is retained by the parents, but more and more physical work is carried out by the children. Many Old Order parents are able to retire from the most demanding labors by their mid-fifties or early sixties.

This released time is then used to assume responsibilities outside the immediate family. The father finds it possible to participate in an increased number of formal and informal meetings with his Amish neighbors. In contrast to many non-Amish who know little about those who live around them, the Old Order are well informed about every part of their community. They are aware of the children's progress in school or any fellow Amishman who has been injured or ill, and they know the general economic condition and progress (or lack of it) of their Amish neighbors. Church work now becomes an activity that occupies more and more of the father's available time. Given the sense of responsibility and concern that each Amishman has for all other members and the collective nature of their society, the well-being of each is a concern of all.

SHUNNING

Any society that seeks to limit the behavior of its members to the extent desired by the Old Order Amish must have some ultimate method of social control. For the Old Order this is the practice of shunning, which has many significant familial ramifications as well as societal considerations. In its widest aspects, shunning means that the member being isolated is totally deprived of communication and interaction with all other Old Order Amish persons. The shunned member eats at a separate table (maybe with the children who have not yet been baptized), and sleeps in a separate bed or room. If the individual is married, marital relations may be terminated. Since Amish individuals receive nearly complete emotional and psychological support from their family and peers, shunning means they are almost totally isolated from contact with others. An Old Order adult interacts with some outsiders; however, this is not of a supportive nature but by design is of limited psychological involvement and conducted with no desire on the part of the Amish for sustained familiarity or deep personal involvement.

A shunned member is in a most uncomfortable position. He may move toward the outside world, but only with the full recognition that this action is further alienating him from his own group and intensifying the emotional and psychological conflict generated by linking more closely with those identified as unacceptable; the alternative, however, demands an equally intense emotional investment. To regain the good graces of family and church, the errant member must acknowledge transgressions by repenting and asking to be readmitted to the church group. The individual must also promise to avoid such pitfalls in the future. This reinstatement is conducted at a regular church meeting and for the shunned member is a most traumatic experience.

Shunning is not used indiscriminately or without the consultation of all church leaders. It is recognized by all Old Order members that this is the most severe form of sanction, short of expulsion, that can be applied. Every effort is made to persuade the individual to correct the errant behavior so that pronouncement of the ban can be avoided. If these means fail, a vote is taken in church the following Sunday and if the vote is unanimous, then and only then is shunning practiced against the transgressor. In some communities if this action is not enough to bring the wayward one back into the group, the elders apply the same treatment to the entire family of the shunned member. Following the pronouncement of shunning, the religious leaders continue their efforts to persuade the sinful member to repent and again enter into full fellowship with the group. Faced with loss of contact with friends and family as well as the immense family suffering, the errant member will usually quickly repent. A shunned member will not be accepted into another Amish community until he has been released from the ban. While other less conservative Mennonite churches do not practice shunning, they will not accept an individual into their membership who is being shunned by the Old Order church.[11]

The anti-Amish behavior that might potentially result in shunning covers personal moral deportment such as infidelity or marriage to a non-Amish individual but may also be initiated for other forms of less personal behavior. The Old Order Amish person who mistreats the soil is, in the eyes of his peers, also sinning.

EXTENDED KINSHIP

As well as having a large number of their own children, Amish parents frequently have others with kinship ties residing in their home, for example a widowed grandparent or unmarried aunt or uncle. The son or daughter of neighbors might be residing with the family as hired help. Sometimes the teacher has moved from another community and finds it necessary to board with a local Amish family living close to the school. While the teacher may be unrelated to the boarding family, there is typically a kinship tie with some family in the school district.

During recent years Amish young men have been able to fulfill their military obligation with two years of alternative service under the Selective Service classification of 1-W. The Amish in Iowa have utilized this by going to another community in the state. For example, a young man from Kalona might to to Milton and live with and work for an Amish family there. Certain requirements must be met such as having the selected site for the alternative service located at least fifty miles from the participant's home. The number of visits the young man may make back to his home community are limited, and records kept of his work are forwarded to the proper authorities. In some cases, the young men work as teachers in other Amish communities.[12]

The Iowa Old Order Amish were particularly pleased when this arrangement was worked out with the Selective Service, since having their young men so far away from home—sometimes in a community without an Amish congregation nearby—presented many problems. If the young man worked in a military hospital, he was required to wear the garb of an orderly, thus losing his most distinctive mark of identification. Oftentimes he was required to cut his hair and, since he wore no beard if not married, then had no outward characteristics to identify him as an Amishman. Living in cities far from home, many young men began to acquire forbidden possessions such as automobiles and television sets. In some cases, Amishmen married nurses whom they met in the hospital, and decided not to return to their home community.[13]

The kinship patterns of the Old Order also include the care of the elderly. As the Amish grow older and retire from active farming, they do not live by themselves but in a small house on the farmstead of one of their children. These are called "grandpa houses." The parents may retire about the time the youngest child marries, and when the first child is born to the young couple, the grandparents often move to the grandpa house and the offspring into the main house. In contrast to many non-Amish societies where preference is given to the oldest child—and in many instances to the oldest male child—for inheritance, the Amish property goes typically to the youngest family member, whether male or female. Some homes have been built to include a separate apartment, complete with kitchen facilities, for the grandparents. Thus the younger family is able to watch over the older couple and help them when necessary. When a grandparent is widowed and needs further care, he or she usually moves in with the young couple. Nursing equipment like hospital beds and wheelchairs are frequently found in the home so the sick members can be cared for properly. Considerable attention is given to the infirm elderly, not only by family members but by others who come to visit frequently. Even non-Amish people visiting in the home for the first time are taken in to meet the elderly person. Regular reports appear in the *Budget* regarding the condition of the sick members.

SEPARATION FROM THE WORLD

Although the Old Order Amish family does not exist in complete isolation from the outside, an integral part of their life-style is separation from the world. They trade at business establishments in nearby communities and seek professional services such as medical care but remain apart from the non-Amish world. Their religious convictions emphasize this deliberate separation, and their life-style is clearly divergent from their non-Amish neighbors. This is echoed in the opinions of non-Amish who view the Old Order as nonconforming people.

A sense of distinctiveness and identity is clearly evident in the clothes of the Old Order, and a member is easily recognized by dress alone. To the non-Amish differences in the brim size of men's hats or the length of the hair (meaningful to the Amish in various communities) are not recognizable, but the distinctive hat and haircut themselves do identify an Amishman. Although not confined just to the Old Order, the women's head covering marks them as belonging to some group within the Mennonite Church. The Amish follow the biblical injunction, "But every woman that prayeth or prophesieth with her head uncovered dishonoureth her head·. . . for this cause ought the woman to have power on her head because of the angels" (I Corinthians 11:5-10). Strict interpretation then makes it mandatory for the woman's head to be covered, but leaves the actual design to the individual group.

In some respects a dual nature then develops: a person is first a member of the Old Order society and second an individual. Knowing that this interpretation is religiously and socially determined and that others of the Amish conviction hold similar views, a sense of solidarity is generated throughout the membership. In addition, the similarity of dress makes contemporaries obvious to the outside world, and an infraction of Amish rules is taken as a reflection on the whole group. Deviation by an Amish person when observed by another is recognized as such even though the two might not be personally acquainted.

In infancy and the early formative years, this sense of being Amish is clearly delineated in the home. In all ways the child is instructed in what is not acceptable. Peer involvements carry a similar constraint, as children know, for example, that they should not play games with dice or cards. During maturation, the young become more and more immersed in Old Order symbolism and traditions and thus systematically exclude any alternatives not acceptable to their life-style.

TRAVELING AND VISITING PATTERNS

Many people presume that because the Amish own only horses and buggies and no automobiles, they are restricted to traveling within a few miles of their own communities. Nothing could be further from the truth, as the Amish are highly mobile in terms of travel. They use buses, both public and chartered, but do most of their traveling by automobile. The standard practice is to "hire" a driver, which actually

Courtesy of the Des Moines Register and Tribune

means hiring both a driver and his vehicle to take them to a nearby community for shopping or medical care, or perhaps even as far away as Ohio or Pennsylvania. In most communities non-Amish owners of van-type vehicles are available on a regular basis for hire by the Amish.

When a relative dies, regardless of the location and relationship, the Amish make a great effort to attend the burial services. Often, when many members of one community wish to attend the funeral of a relative or friend in another area, they charter a commercial bus. One Amishman takes charge, checks on the number of people going, and presents the bus driver with a list of people and directions for locating their farms. As each person or family is picked up, they have money

"WELL FANCY MEETING YOU HERE."

ready to pay the driver. Each individual or family will bring along a large lunch basket, which contains ample food to tide them over until they reach their destination. If they are traveling for several days, they will stop at Amish settlements along the way where they will be fed and can spend the night. The Amish are proud of the fact that they can travel from coast to coast and not buy a meal in a restaurant or pay for a night's lodging. One Amishman, commenting on this practice, chuckled and said, "We call that Mennoniting around!"[14]

A limited amount of travel would fall into the category of entertainment or vacation time. The Amish believe that visiting natural sites such as the Grand Canyon and going to zoos to see the creatures

71

that God has created are natural and good. These activities are limited, however, because a trip means work undone on the farm and also involves expense. With large families, the costs are multiplied many times. Even so, many Amish families do travel and thoroughly delight in visiting other states. One family took their children to St. Louis and while there visited Forest Park Zoo. In commenting on the trip, the mother was amused, saying that her family proved to be about as much of an attraction at the zoo as the animals. Another Iowa Amish couple wished to take a trip to California. Locating a non-Amish family that also wanted to go, they arranged to have their camping trailer pulled along at the cost of seven cents a mile. The couple was very proud of their arrangement, as otherwise the cost would have been twelve cents a mile. They visited Disneyland and many other attractions and in total traveled some 4,000 miles.[15]

A current practice of the Amish is to buy a bus ticket called "Ameripass" that entitles one person to sixty days of bus travel anywhere in the continental United States and lower Canada. The cost is reasonable, and all major bus companies honor the arrangement. The traveling days do not have to be consecutive; therefore, an Amishman can travel to another Amish community, stay for several days, and then travel to the next location. With their frugal spending habits, this is an ideal way to travel since they will seldom need to buy meals or lodging.

MEDICAL PRACTICES

In most non-Amish families the care of the sick and the injured has moved steadily toward the use of professional people and care. Doctors, clinics, hospitals, and other specialized services have gradually eroded the importance of home treatment. For the Old Order this movement has been much slower, since they still provide considerable medical .care at home, particularly for the elderly, and believe in assorted home remedies. The Amish have no trained physicians among their own population, so must rely totally on outside personnel and facilities. They do, however, make use of medical doctors and hospital facilities when they feel it is necessary.

In general, the Amish favor what they refer to as "the natural way." In Iowa, they reflect that philosophy by making extensive use of chiropractors for preventive medicine as well as treatment for an illness or disability. It is common practice for an entire Amish family to visit a chiropractor for adjustments or treatments on a regular basis. The visit may take place every two weeks or monthly and include babies as young as five months plus older children ranging in age from toddlers to youngsters in their teens. The visit also represents a special trip to town, which the older family members enjoy, and perhaps includes a treat such as a stop for an ice cream cone on the way home. Several chiropractors in Amish communities have stated that they believe they are regarded as family physicians and that the Amish come to them for most of their health problems. The Amish will also call the chiropractor to come to their home to give them an adjustment.[16]

The Iowa Amish frequently patronize the chiropractic clinics in Canistota and Marion, South Dakota, usually staying for one week. In fact, it is not unusual for a vanload of six to eight from a particular community to travel to the clinic for treatments. Frequently during the winter months retired Amish, usually men, will travel to Hot Springs, Arkansas, or Boulder, Montana, for the hot mineral baths. Also in Boulder, patients seek the therapeutic effects of radium by entering the mines for a specified period. These treatments are regarded in much the same light as the chiropractic adjustments in that it is more natural than taking drugs or tranquilizers or undergoing surgery.

Some Amish health practices fall into the category of folk medicine or healing. Foot rubbing is such a practice and is believed by some to have highly therapeutic value. Practitioners of this method claim that the human foot contains the nerve ends for every section of the human body and that through proper manipulation and massage, a person knowledgeable in this practice can determine the cause of a person's illness and cure the disorder. One Amish family reported that their three-month-old baby had been continually bothered with colic and as a result had been very fussy. The baby also, in the mother's opinion, was not gaining enough weight nor was he very responsive. Worried that something was seriously wrong, the husband secured a book on foot rubbing and began to massage the infant's feet according to the directions. Within a short time the baby stopped fussing, began to gain weight, and overall appeared to be in better health. The parents are convinced that the foot rubbing brought about the change.[17]

The *Budget* contains numerous advertisements for nerve remedies that carry the connotation of patent medicines. "Kalms" is advertised regularly as a tablet that is "nature's tranquilizer." The ad describes this product as "safe, gentle, nontoxic . . . made entirely from plants and flowers." Another regularly advertised product is Carrot Oil, suggested for "eyes, nerves, heart, rickets, colds and run down [condition]." In the Iowa communities, a favorite of many Old Order people is PoHo Oil. The ingredients are listed as "peppermint oil in a liquid petrolatum base." The label warns that the product is not "implied as a cure under any condition," yet lists directions for both internal and external use. These range from putting "15 drops in a small quantity of water for stomach or bowel trouble" to sprinkling a few drops on a handkerchief and inhaling the fumes as often as possible for hay fever.

The Old Order resist the use of immunization shots and are critical of the use of pills such as aspirin. They do, however, frequently take vitamin supplements; they particularly believe that vitamin C helps to prevent and cure colds. Their reasoning regarding shots and pills has a direct relationship to a distinction drawn between a natural product and an artificial one. Vitamins are found naturally in foods and are consequently acceptable, while other medicines are suspected as being drugs and producing a harmful effect on the body.

Home remedies also form a part of the Amish medical practices. Most garden plots contain a section devoted to medicinal plants and herbs. Some substances are brewed as teas and some blended as ointments; in this sense, the practices of the Old Order appear to be similar to those of the early American pioneers. The use of poultices for infections and mustard plasters and chest rubs for colds and pneumonia reflect family treatments of an earlier age. One Amish family told of friends that regularly treated their daughter's asthma attacks by preparing a concoction of lemonade and herbs. They stated that the liquid relieved the child's breathing difficulty almost immediately.[18]

When the Amish become seriously ill or a person is badly injured, there is usually no hesitation in using the services of a medical doctor. The Amish have no religious rules against modern medicine, and their use of these services depends upon economic considerations as well as other factors. People with broken bones are taken immediately to a physician for treatment. There is a high rate of accidents on Amish farms in connection with power take-off units, which are frequently homemade devices lacking proper safety equipment. Amish boys sometimes get broken or badly mangled arms as a result of catching their clothing in the power take-off and being pulled into the machinery. Another example concerns a young Amish farmer in the Milton community who suffered a severe head injury as the result of a fall. He was taken by ambulance to Bloomfield and from there to the University Hospitals at Iowa City. He received numerous examinations by specialists and was in the intensive care unit for a short period. In such cases there is usually no question but that the best medical facilities and specialists will be utilized. In other instances, consulting a medical doctor might be called a second line of service. If the disability does not respond to a chiropractor's treatments or home remedies, the patient will no doubt be taken to a physician.

Also a part of Amish medical practices is the "laying on of hands" and the offering of prayers as a way of treating the sick. These approaches may be the same or used separately; sometimes they are combined with visits to a physician. Yet at other times parents will combine home medical treatment with outside medical assistance. From time to time in the *Budget* testimonials will appear telling of a person whose illness had not responded to medical treatment and who subsequently returned home and was cured by prayer and the laying on of hands by local religious officials. The following case illustrates the point.

In the Kalona community, a five-year-old boy contacted what was later believed to have been either polio or spinal meningitis. At the onset of the illness, however, the parents did not take the boy to a medical doctor, so there was no specific diagnosis. The parents first observed that something was wrong with their son when he appeared to drag one foot and on several occasions fell down for no apparent reason. Previously, the child had fallen several times while playing and the parents though he might have suffered a back injury. The next day the boy appeared to be partially paralyzed from the waist down but could still walk with difficulty. He was taken to a local chiropractor who told the parents that the boy had symptoms of polio. This produced consternation, as many Amish friends had advised the parents not to take their son to the hospital if he did have the disease. These friends claimed that several other Amish children who had contacted polio had responded better to chiropractic treatments than to hospitalization and care of a physician. Heeding this advice, the parents took their son to the chiropractor for a series of treatments. The boy became increasingly ill and the paralysis increased until it severely affected his breathing. By this time he had lost about twenty pounds and was completely helpless.[19]

Four weeks after the start of the problem the boy seemed to be responding to treatment, and the numbness began to dissipate. Within a few days he could move his left arm and the two smallest fingers on his left hand, then his entire arm. In two weeks he could lift his head while lying on his stomach. Several weeks later, at the suggestion of the chiropractor, the parents took their son to an osteopath who diagnosed the illness as spinal meningitis and expressed surprise that the boy was still alive. However, in light of his progress, the prognosis was for complete recovery in time. Thirteen weeks after the ordeal began, the boy could stand without assistance and walk with a somewhat awkward gait. Today the child appears to have completely recovered with the exception of a barely perceptible limp.[20]

The parents attribute the boy's recovery to the power of God.

Reports of his illness and subsequent progress were printed in the *Budget* and elicited prayers from Amish all over the country. The parents believe that God heard all their prayers and responded to the pleas by making their son well. [21]

Many Old Order people have sight deficiencies and find it necessary to wear corrective lenses. Amish children often wear thick eyeglasses, and although no studies have been made in this particular area, it seems that extreme nearsightedness is becoming more common. Dental care presents little concern for Amish parents unless a specific problem or some discomfort develops. Regular dental checks are not considered important.

Amish women use the facilities of a physician for childbirth, and many babies are born in hospitals. Although some are born at home, a physician is usually in attendance and the training and use of midwives does not appear to be present in any Amish communities. Prenatal care is not thought to be important unless the wife has had difficulty with a previous birth. Once the baby is born, Amish mothers are anxious to go home, and they traditionally have shorter hospitalization than non-Amish. The major consideration is money, but another is that the mother will have a hired girl when she goes home and therefore can continue her rest period within the circle of the family.

In an effort to avoid the cost of the hospital but still ensure the presence of a physician, some Amish families have been known to

THE SUNDAY VISIT.

Photo by Joan Liffring Zug

arrive at the doctor's office just in time for the birth of the child. The father might call ahead to make certain the doctor would be in his office, but otherwise no preparations would be made for hospitalization. If the timing was right, there would be no time to move the mother to the hospital and the doctor would deliver her in his office. Then if there were no complications, both mother and baby could go directly home and hospitalization costs would be avoided.

Amish leaders indicate that rising health costs are one of the major problems they face. They do not subscribe to any health insurance programs because they feel that it would violate the biblical injunction, "Be ye not unequally yoked together with unbelievers . . ." (II Corinthians 6:14). Certainly another consideration is economic since regular insurance premiums would mean a considerable drain on a family with seven to nine children. Although the Amish policy of mutual aid helps families who have large medical bills, even with this assistance Amish leaders see medical and hospital costs as an ever-growing problem. Some believe these constantly rising costs represent one of the most serious problems they will face in the foreseeable future.[22]

As a general rule, the Amish appear to be a healthy and vigorous group who spend a great deal of time outdoors doing physical labor. It is rare indeed to see a sallow-faced person, and children and adults alike have ruddy, beautiful, blemish-free complexions that reflect their

general good health. Amish people are typically short or average in height. Some mental retardation occurs but since no studies have been made in this area, there is no reason to believe that they have a higher rate of retardation than the non-Amish population. However, there has been high incidence of several recessive genetic disorders among certain Amish populations. Dr. Victor A. McKusick, a Johns Hopkins scientist, noted in 1964 that among 45,000 Amish in the United States and Canada, eighty instances had been found of a form of dwarfism that resulted in hair so sparse and fine that the female victims could not braid their hair in typical Amish fashion. Also noted was another form of dwarfism characterized by six-fingered hands and sometimes by hearts having only three chambers instead of four. This condition, called the Ellis-van Creveld syndrome, was found among Amish living in Lancaster County, Indiana. Moreover, McKusick stated that researchers had observed a high frequency of hemophilia, an unusual form of anemia, and a form of muscular dystrophy, apparently due to the high in-breeding conditions of the Amish.[23]

Mental illness is present among the Iowa Amish, but it is difficult if not impossible to know the number of people affected by such problems. The Amish care for their own and very infrequently place a member in a mental hospital or go to a mental health institute for assistance. Amish authority John Hostetler believes that the rate of suicide among the Amish is as high, if not higher, than among the non-Amish population but bases most of his studies on Amish populations in Pennsylvania, Ohio, and other eastern areas. Interviews among Iowa Amish groups have indicated only a limited number of suicides, ranking well below the general population average.[24]

SUMMARY

The constraining nature of Amish society is all-pervasive, and its influence is felt from the cradle to the grave. The individual is influenced early by the home environment and later by the total Amish society as he interacts with nonfamily members and Amish peers as well as with people in the outside world. These characteristics are not just restrictive but totally supporting as well. Growing children are nurtured by family and culture in such a way that they have few if any needs demanding response from the non-Amish society. Thus being Amish means living in a closely interwoven society that links religious, familial, societal, educational, and vocational beliefs into a complete whole. Totally immersed in the Old Order traditions and participating in a society where members have the resources and desire to continually provide for each other, the Amish member experiences a sense of security that few non-Amish ever know. The degree of constraint on the individual is mitigated by a sense of separateness from the outside world and also by the freedom to relocate in another Old Order community where certain conditions might be slightly different and therefore more to the liking of a particular family.

Non-Amish people sometimes seek out different types of associations or clubs that take the place of the family, but for the Old Order such associations do not exist and familial interaction and responsibility provide the ultimate form of involvement.

ON THE MOVE.

Courtesy of the Des Moines Register and Tribune

CHAPTER SIX **Mobility**

From the beginning of their history the Amish have been a highly mobile people. From observing Old Order Amish settlement patterns in Iowa and other parts of the Midwest, it can be seen that mobility is still a part of their life-style. Since the early 1950s the Old Order have initiated fourteen new settlements in Iowa, Missouri, and Minnesota. A major new Iowa group can be found in the Milton-Pulaski area, which the Amish refer to as the Milton community. The selection of this particular site, the procedure involved in the establishment of a new community, and the resulting rules and organization provide deeper understanding of the Old Order Amish as well as highlighting the reasons for their success as a religious, utopian society. The process also provides an opportunity to study the Old Order Amish and their relationship to the general non-Amish community. Moreover, a close examination of the expansion and mobility policies of the Amish allows for meaningful comparisons with other important utopian societies. In briefly analyzing these features in two other Iowa groups, the Amana

and New Communities

Colonies and the Icarians, it appears that only the Old Order Amish have provided for—and continue to provide—some degree of flexibility and choice to their members in regard to place of residence.

INITIATING NEW SETTLEMENTS

Although the Old Order Amish start new settlements for a variety of reasons, the dominant motivation is economic. Like all other agriculturists, they are faced with constantly rising land values throughout the eastern United States as well as in well-established midwestern communities. In Lancaster County, Pennsylvania, once the center of Amish life in America, much land is selling for well over $1,500 per acre. In Kalona at a farm sale in early 1973, an eighty-acre farm brought $1,025 per acre. The Amish need for additional land is constant because sons and daughters from the large families are continually establishing new households. Unwilling and many times unable to purchase land at these high prices, they have sought to establish communities in areas where land is cheap and yet available in sufficient quantities that a sizable settlement may develop.

Other reasons for resettlement of Old Order Amish families are highly diverse. Personal dispute between family or nonfamily members may serve as a catalyst to consideration of a move. In Iowa, controversies with public school officials have prompted a number of Buchanan County families to move to Wisconsin.[1] Some families may feel that their local parochial school is inadequate and move so that their children may receive a better education. Still others resettle in a new community because other members of their family — possibly a father, brother, or son — had gone there previously and the family desired to live closer together.[2]

Still another consideration is that as the size of the older Amish communities increases, there may be a breakdown between members and sometimes even within family groups. Parents occasionally find it difficult to enforce rules and regulations regarding behavior. A move to a new community, particularly during the early years when the population is relatively small, allows the family to pull closer together and makes it easier to enforce rules and apply discipline. Thus a reduction in community size helps to reassert parental authority.[3]

There are also within Amish society certain marginal individuals who deviate sufficiently from acceptable behavior so that they are looked upon as undesirable. Perhaps some parents have failed to discipline their children properly or are not sufficiently restrictive. Perhaps some church members have continual money or management problems and must frequently be assisted by others. Some may not share the general belief that parochial schools are superior to public schools. Any of these actions may place a questionable household on the periphery of the Amish community and, seeking more acceptance, that family may move to a new area.

Since they rely on horses and buggies, the Amish must live fairly close to a trading center as well as to each other. An Amishman could not, for example, conveniently live fifteen miles away from the nearest town, as too much of his time would be taken traveling back and forth. As the young people marry, they are finding it increasingly difficult to locate land for sale within the necessary distance of other Amish families and trade facilities. The only choice is to seek land in another community, which in some instances means initiating a new settlement.

Because of the obvious need for additional land, all members realize that expansion is vital; therefore, the Amish regard new communities as positive experiences and make no attempt to prevent their population from growing. The Amish in the new communities maintain harmonious relations with the older settlements, and much interaction takes place in the form of visiting. Conversely, if the Amish had looked upon each new settlement as something of a split or rift within their faith, the consequences would have been highly detrimental over the years and many more schisms probably would have developed.

While there may be varying degrees of conservatism regarding the use of tractors or domestic appliances, each community adheres to the basic principles of the Old Order Amish faith. When an Amishman from Arthur, Illinois, moves to Milton, Iowa, for example, he knows that, given prior approval by the Milton bishop, he will be accepted totally with all rights and privileges generally accorded to members of the group. He and his family will relocate on a farm that encompasses roughly the same number of acres as the farm they left behind. They will move into a house that is similar in size and arrangement to their old one; the Amish housewife will decorate the new home in the same fashion as the old, and it will reflect the same austere life-style. The farm work schedule will go on almost unchanged from the previous location. The lay of the land might vary, but the same crop rotation system will be implemented and the same general livestock program will be followed. On Sunday morning, the family will hitch up their buggies and head down the road to their neighbor's farm. There they will gather with other Amish families to hear the same sermons and prayers and they will sing the same familiar songs. In short, little has changed for this Amish family because they moved from Illinois to Iowa. Matters that would be of vital significance to non-Amish families, such as the public schools, community cultural and recreational opportunities, and transportation and general shopping facilities, do not concern the Amish. Given the built-in security that their society provides and the subsequent elimination of considerable stress, Amish families find it far less difficult to make decisions regarding moves than non-Amish families and therefore find the move requires minimal adjustments.

The first step in considering a new settlement may be taken by one or more people. In the case of the Milton community, a Buchanan County Amishman contacted four others also living in that area regarding the possibility of starting a new settlement. The five shared several concerns ranging from the conservatism of the Buchanan County group to the feeling that perhaps that community had grown so large that some parents were having difficulty controlling their youngsters. The Amishmen also agreed that it would be good to find an area where large amounts of cheaper land would be available than that for sale in Buchanan County, and they began to travel throughout the Midwest searching for possible sites. On a trip to Missouri they were told that Missouri and Kalona Amish previously had considered land around Milton. They visited that vicinity and liked the appearance of the area. Later they returned to Milton to look at specific farms and in 1968 made the final decision to locate there.[4]

THE MILTON COMMUNITY

Milton is a small, quiet town located in the southeastern part of the state. Like dozens of other rural Iowa comminities, it has a single main street with a handful of businesses scattered along either side. A number of deserted buildings give evidence that at one time the community was larger and more prosperous. Most of the homes are older, but occasionally a new ranch style house has been built among the old, a typical characteristic of a small midwestern community. The tempo of life appears relaxed, particularly during the winter months as local farmers come into the hardware store and stand around the heating stove exchanging stories and catching up on the latest gossip. Milton is a friendly, rather tranquil town, whose people cater mainly to the farmers residing in the rolling countryside that surrounds the community.

The Milton area was particularly well suited to Amish settlement for several reasons. Some land was selling for as low as $150 per acre in 1968, while the average price per acre was $200. In both Davis and Van Buren counties there were many farms for sale that ranged between 100 and 120 acres. Apparently farm sizes in those counties had remained small because they had been among the first areas to be settled in Iowa during the 1830s and 1840s, and the original homesteads frequently contained around 100 acres. Unlike most other Iowa farmers, many landowners there did not enlarge the original holdings because of farming methods and the hilly terrain. These small acreages were ideal for the Old Order Amish with their horse-drawn equipment, and they approximated the size of farms in Kalona and in Buchanan County. Units of approximately 100 acres provided each Amish family with a house, barn, and other outbuildings; whereas purchasing a larger farmstead of 200 or 300 acres would have necessitated the dividing and reselling of a part of the land. It would then have been necessary to erect buildings on the other half of the original holding, which would have involved time and money.[5]

Milton's population is about 600, while Pulaski has about 300 inhabitants. Bloomfield, located about twenty miles northwest of Milton, has a population of about 2,500. By settling close to small rural communities, the Amish find there is less to tempt their children in terms of amusement, shopping centers, and general commercial activities. Since there are fewer problems of delinquency and vandalism among Amish youth in small communities than in larger ones, the Milton area appeared highly desirable.[6]

Before the original five families moved, however, they believed that they should select a religious leader. A bishop at Jamesport, Missouri, was contacted and agreed to join them. When starting a new community, many Amish wait until the move has been made and then make the selection of a minister or a bishop. In the case of Milton, however, the group agreed that it would be best to have the matter settled ahead of time.[7]

The six families met in a local real estate agent's home in Milton and drew up the rules to govern their community. These covered religious, educational, agricultural, and domestic issues that might arise within that particular area. One of the decisions, for example, was that kerosene kitchen ranges and refrigerators could be used, but unlike in Kalona, no propane gas appliances. Further questions and difficulties that arose would usually be decided by the bishop. No doubt he counseled with the other men, but the ultimate decision was his. During the first two years of the Milton settlement non-Amish neighbors were invited to Amish weddings. Eventually, however, the bishop made the decision that only Amish people should be included because the attendance had grown too large.[8]

A rather unusual situation developed as a result of the bishop's rule that members could use only kerosene as a source of energy. The Amish had heard that kerosene refrigerators were available, but they did not know precisely where. They approached the local hardware dealer and requested that he try to locate a manufacturer so they could order several models. Following a long search, the dealer was not able to find a source in the United States but did hear about a firm in Brazil. Several units were ordered and when the shipment arrived, everyone was in for a surprise. The price was considerably higher than a traditional model, roughly $600, and they were made out of heavy plastic. The biggest surprise, however, was that the instructions for assembling the units were written in Portuguese![9]

Once the initial six families set down the original rules, all those settling in the Milton area later were expected to conform. When considering a move, the usual procedure is for a family to visit the selected community and acquaint themselves with the governing restrictions. If they believe they can abide by these rules, a move is probably made. If the family members are not satisfied with the arrangements, however, they would no doubt look around for another community more to their liking. It is also apparent from the frequent moves made by many Amish that they either do not care to live with certain restrictions or believe they might live more comfortably elsewhere. One example of the search for a more compatible community involved a family that had moved to Milton during the first year or two of that settlement. Several years later, however, they moved on to a new community in another state, but still in the Middle West. Movement both into and out of Iowa can be observed through accounts in the *Budget,* and this family made three moves in five years. They were obviously more mobile than most, and inquiry revealed that the Amish father had the unacceptable habit of smoking. Apparently he had hoped to find a community where the taboo against tobacco was not quite so strong. It was the feeling of some Amish that he had apparently done so in his latest location and would probably remain there.[10]

The original six Milton families exercised some control over others considering a move into the area. Obviously, if members of the new community had left their previous homes to avoid certain members within that settlement, they would resist having these families move to their new area. To prevent that from happening and also to retain some control over the future membership and hence direction of the community, certain ''agreements'' were laid down. The major real estate agents involved in the initial land transactions agreed not to sell land to any Amish families not approved by the initial six. The bishop also remained an extremely influential figure in determining whether or not new families would be approved. In this way the future direction of the settlement was controlled through the admission of new members.[11]

Following the initial settlement, the Milton community has grown rapidly. In 1974 approximately fifty families were residing there and if trends continue, the community will expand as long as land is available. Starting with one church district, it has been necessary to divide the group into two, the North District and the South District, with Highway 2 marking the boundary. The bishop from the North District also serves the South District, but both provide several ministers who assist him in his duties. A new bishop undoubtedly will be selected for the latter group.

After more than five years of settlement the Amish reaction to their venture is very positive. Many have commented that their community has grown much more rapidly than they had anticipated and that they are happy with their decision to locate there. Moreover, they feel that a good relationship exists with the general community and that they have been well received.[12]

The non-Amish community reaction is not so clearly discernible and appears to have shifted even during the short period that the Plain People have resided in Davis and Van Buren counties. The initial reaction of many was one of enthusiasm as they realized that some farmsteads that had stood empty for years would be inhabited. Apparently it was thought that this would bring some degree of economic rejuvenation to an otherwise semidepressed agricultural area. As the first families began to move in, however, it became apparent that the Amish would not use many of the community services. Relying on horses, the Amish eliminated any need for gasoline as well as for high-priced farm equipment such as tractors, combines, or pickups. The Amish way of life meant that the rural electrification program would have fewer subscribers, as would the rural telephone exchange. In other words, the Amish might possibly have a restrictive economic effect on the community rather than an expansive one. The negativism became further apparent as residents realized that community functions such as future school enrollment and local church attendance would be affected. Although many farms had stood empty before Amish families moved in, the purchases precluded any non-Amish families from buying the land and participating in community-provided services. Overall, however, most residents appear to favor the settlement and in general believe that the Amish make "good neighbors." Moreover, they are regarded unanimously as honest, hardworking people. The negative aspects begin to surface when the topic of conversation shifts to the overall economic effects of large-scale Amish settlement in the area.[13]

THE BLOOMFIELD SETTLEMENT

An unusual feature of the Milton-Pulaski settlement is the quasi-separate Old Order Amish group located west of Bloomfield.[14] Four related families moved there from Buchanan County in the spring of 1971, and for almost three years no other families came to the area. During this period contact was maintained, however, with other Old Order Amish groups, particularly at Kalona. In the spring of 1974, families from Fortuna and Clark, Missouri, as well as from the nearby Milton community joined the group and for the first time the settlement moved beyond a family unit. In its first few years, the Bloomfield group presented a very unusual situation that does not often develop. With all the families related, it was not possible for the traditional social and courtship activities to take place.

In the spring of 1973 one of the families relocated in the Pulaski area. This placed them within the boundaries of the Milton Old Order community. The family's oldest children had reached courting age and this fact reportedly strongly influenced the decision to move to a larger, more traditional community. It is doubtful if the remaining Bloomfield families — because of the insular nature of Amish life — would have remained intact if other nonrelated families had not settled in the area. In a typical Amish settlement there are sufficient young people to provide a social life for the young nonmarried members, which leads to courtship activities and eventually marriage. Each community must be somewhat self-sufficient in providing marriage partners for its members. Although Bloomfield is located only about twenty miles from the Pulaski-Milton group, that distance was sufficient to severely limit social interaction between the young people.[15] In the past many Amish settlements have failed because they were unable to achieve sufficient membership to fulfill the mating requirement.[16]

SUPERSTITIONS

As with many other minority groups, the Old Order Amish must tolerate superstitious beliefs and myths regarding their society. In the first years of settlement in any area, these are particularly evident. One of these alleged facts is that the color blue has special significance for the Plain People, a myth that appears to surface wherever there are Amish settlements. The Milton Amish reject this idea with the comment that if there is an abundance of blue houses, blue barns, or blue interiors, it probably means that there has been a sale on blue paint at the local hardware store. To illustrate how widespread this delusion has become, a Milton Old Order Amishman related that his brother had even read in a *Lassie* book that a family, trying to decide on a color for the barn, decided to paint it blue like the Amish. Another widespread myth is that an Amish family paints their front door or front gatepost blue when they have a daughter of marriageable age, as if to advertise the fact. Yet another rumor is that the front parlor curtains will be crossed in a particular fashion if the family has a daughter of marrying age. The latter is particularly humorous since most Amish housewives do not hang curtains at their windows. The Amish react to such misconceptions with good humor and patience, and at times seem to enjoy the situation for the nonsense that it is.[17]

When the first families moved into the Milton area, many purchased completely modernized homes. It was necessary to remove the electric wires, disconnect the furnaces, and take out the telephones. Probably because of these actions, many non-Amish residents assumed that bathroom facilities were also forbidden. The rumor circulated then and continues to be heard that the Amish had to block off the regular doorway to the bathroom and build an exterior entry. In other words the facilities could be used but the access had to be from the outside. When asked about this matter, one Amishman responded that he too had heard the rumor and added, "Now wouldn't that be a foolish thing to do?"[18]

Another persistent story that has circulated widely in the Milton area is that the Amish started the community primarily to counter inbreeding. Given the insulated nature of their society, continual intermarriage between Old Order families has produced some genetic disorders of which dwarfism is probably the most widely recognized. Many non-Amish families in the Milton area have cited this as a reason for the beginning of that community. This reason has never been discussed by an Amish family, however, as a possible rationale for their movement to the area. There seems to be no evidence to support this notion, as some Amish families moved to the Milton area because parents, sisters, or brothers had previously moved there. Within a short time after the settlement started, many interrelated families were living in the area.[19]

THE MOBILITY FACTOR

With their practice of creating new settlements at frequent intervals, the Old Order Amish possess a quality of flexibility that should be emphasized strongly in analyzing their past history and present-day success. If longevity is a sign of success, and it is usually regarded as such in considering most utopian societies, the Amish are one of two utopian groups that have been in existence for almost 300 years.[20] Throughout their history they have had the alternative of migration to a new area—a new continent, a new country, or simply a new community. The slight, sometimes microscopic, change that then takes place within the group gives the Amish a degree of flexibility that enables them to accommodate individual differences but yet remain within the general confines of their Old Order beliefs. To the Amish, then, mobility has brought stability.

Aside from the economic considerations of solving their immediate land problems, the freedom to move and to do so frequently provides the Amish population with a "safety valve." The reasons for relocating in a new community may be many and varied: unhappiness with a strict bishop and a desire for a slightly more liberal attitude toward fraternization with non-Amish; a desire to work in areas outside agriculture such as carpentry, cinder block laying, or house moving; or perhaps a desire to purchase a tractor for fieldwork. In establishing a new group, the rules are redefined and there is a realignment of leadership. Because of the almost sovereign position of the bishop within the individual church districts, the new community has a degree of freedom to restructure the life-style. On the other hand once the community has become settled, the guidelines are obvious, so that other Amish families can readily determine whether or not they would fit into a particular community.

It should be emphasized, however, that the change will never be major. Although there is no overall authority or regulation imposed from the top down, each group clearly recognizes the limits of change. To remain in the Old Order group, no compromise or modification of major religious beliefs will be tolerated even though local custom may vary.

MOBILITY AMONG OTHER UTOPIAN GROUPS

In comparing the Old Order Amish to other utopian groups that have existed in Iowa as well as in other parts of the United States, this flexibility or built-in mechanism for minor change leads to significant contrasts between the societies. Two utopian groups that located in Iowa, the Amana Colonies and the Icarians, provide a contrast to the Old Order Amish in this respect. The Amana group, originating in Germany in the early 1700s, descended from eighteenth-century German mystics and pietists. In 1842 they migrated to the United states and settled in New York State where they started a settlement called Ebenezer. There the Amana people adopted a communal way of life. Within a short time their agricultural and craft operations prospered and they needed more land, so they looked to western regions like Iowa. In 1855 they arrived in the Hawkeye State and settled seven villages. Eventually the society purchased 30,000 acres of contiguous land and reestablished their various craft operations along with their agricultural activities. They named their new home, Amana, which means "Believe faithfully." Once relocated in Iowa, they made no attempt to expand, either because of population pressure or by establishing new colonies. The Amanas attempted to isolate themselves from outsiders by developing their own industries and becoming nearly self-sufficient in their economic life. In 1932, experiencing severe economic problems, the people voted to abandon their communal life. They organized the colony on a capitalistic basis and each member received stock in the corporation. Continuing to maintain their corporate business structure, the Amana Colonies today operate a thriving business and are a major tourist attraction in the Midwest.[21]

Prior to the 1932 economic change, however, there was little flexibility or deviance within the group. For the Amanite who was unhappy with the work to be performed or the communal living arrangements, there was only one drastic alternative — to leave the colonies. If this occurred, the person was considered an outcast by the remaining members. It was not possible to move to another Amana settlement, as none existed, nor was it possible to initiate a new group. Because few people left Amana, the dissidents remained within the system and probably agitated, openly or inadvertently, for change in their life-style. No doubt these people had little zeal to maintain the system or to contribute much to it in terms of their own labor. Thus there was no safety valve available to the Amana inhabitants during their communal history.

The Icarians who settled in Iowa in 1856 shared a common life-style with the Amanas as well as experiencing many similar problems. The Icarians originated in France in the early 1800s, adopting the socialistic philosophy of Étienne Cabet. Hoping to put Cabet's theories into practice, the group emigrated to the United States to establish "Icaria," the name of the imaginary community that Cabet had described in his writings. The initial settlement in Texas failed, and the group then moved to Nauvoo, Illinois, the former home of the Mormons. After a short stay in Illinois they moved to Adams County, Iowa, to attempt once more to create their ideal community. Communal living and hard work paid off for the Icarians; within twenty years after they had relocated in Iowa, they had erased their land debt and greatly improved their standard of living.[22]

Unlike the Amanas, however, the Icarians did not attempt to isolate themselves. In fact, many efforts were made to develop cordial relations with their non-Icarian neighbors, particularly the citizens of Corning. The Icarians, a well-educated and culturally appreciative people, presented operas, lectures, and plays to which they invited the townspeople. At one time an Icarian member held French classes while another taught German. Yet another person presented classes in electricity. Other Corning citizens took music lessons from the talented Icarians as well as studying art at the colony.[23]

However, prosperity brought many problems. The Icarian young people, associating more and more with outsiders, began to develop the same acquisitive tastes for material goods. Paid no money for their labors within the colony, they became increasingly restless. Eventually a major division occurred between the younger and older believers over matters such as the admission of new members, extension of voting rights to women, and economic expansion through industrial programs. Unable to solve their differences, many younger members left the group and formed a second colony, also named Icaria. The older people then took the name "New Icaria" and relocated a short distance from the original site. The disagreements were never solved, however, and within a short time many younger members had left Iowa to join a group in California, and the older ones were forced to disband. [24]

Although the Icarians did split into two groups under extreme duress, the separation did little or nothing to eliminate harsh feelings or placate the grievances. As with the Amanites there was no legitimate way that the Icarians could redefine the rules and agitate for change within their society. The Icarian member, unhappy with his role in the socialistic community, could only push for a split in membership with all the accompanying reprisals and negative feelings or leave the group completely.

Although it is not within the confines of this study to deal with the American utopian movement in its broadest sense, it is worthwhile to note that major groups like the Rappites and Owenites as well as the Aurora and Bethel communities were similar to the Amanas and Icarians in terms of their single community organization. The Shakers, although increasing to eighteen colonies during the decade before the Civil War, allowed for little autonomy or deviance among the individual groups. The center of Shakerism was New Lebanon, New York; there the central ministry appointed the branch ministries of the other colonies. Each colony (branch ministry) contained families of approximately fifty people. Unlike the Amish settlements, however, the new Shaker colonies developed as more converts joined the order and in turn created a need for additional land and living facilities. Although some deviancy was undoubtedly allowed within the separate colonies, these groups were not regarded as autonomous but remained fully under the control and guidance of the central ministry. [25]

CONCLUSION

In assessing the history and present-day success of the Old Order Amish, it is somewhat paradoxical that a people who are so seemingly immobile — given their unchanging ways and their nineteenth-century form of transportation — would be in reality a highly mobile population. As long as land remains available and they continue to move and establish new communities, the Amish will have a safety valve for their discontent. Dissidents will be able to continue moving out of the communities where they are dissatisfied, resettling in areas where they feel more in harmony with the membership. If, however, conditions arise that restrict this opportunity, Amish society could undergo significant change.

A MOMENT OF FRIGHT.

Courtesy of the Des Moines Register and Tribune

C H A P T E R   S E V E N

In American society during the past several decades, a tendency has developed to diminish parental responsibilities in the area of social and educational development. Increasingly parents are turning over to nonfamily agencies the responsibility of caring for and educating their offspring. Preschool programs, day-care centers, and summer camps as well as the public schools have been assuming an ever-increasing role. Moreover, children of school age are spending less and less time at home. As school units have been consolidated and have thus grown increasingly larger, children are bused to school, leaving home at an

The School Controversy

earlier hour in the morning and arriving home later at night. More and more extracurricular activities are available to young people, which means that once again they are absent from the home for long periods and parents have less involvement in educational activities.

The Old Order Amish, with their view of limited parochial education, have experienced none of these developments. The Amish think of the school as an extension of their daily lives; they plan it, provide for its facilities and teachers, participate in its programs, and are totally responsible for its content and conduct. The school board is

95

composed of Amish fathers who no doubt originally paid for and constructed the school building itself. Amish mothers are involved because they help maintain the building by frequent cleanings and the application of an occasional coat of paint. All Amish families in the school district have some control over the hiring of teachers and other policy matters. The school is, in other words, an integral part of their lives.

The involvement of the entire family in school matters underscores the attitudes that the Amish hold toward education of their young. Of all the issues that face them today education is perhaps the most controversial and vital. They insist on a separate school setting, away from the centers of population, that does not include school consolidation or busing. In recent years they have also insisted on hiring their own members as teachers. The Amish believe unequivocably in an eighth grade education but not beyond, because they believe that the values taught in high school conflict with their own central religious concepts. Parents stress humility and simplicity and reject worldly ideas and behavior. High schools on the other hand generally emphasize intellectual attainment, social integration and interaction, individual achievement, and competitiveness, some of which are regarded as sinful by Amish parents. Moreover, high school attendance involves some form of transportation, probably busing, and sustained interaction with non-Amish youngsters. The curriculum itself presents problems, as some courses include material that violates Amish religious beliefs, such as the theory of evolution and any study of the human body. Frequently, modern equipment such as television sets are used to present classroom material.

The Amish recognize full well the dangers inherent for them in the public school system, and on this issue they will not compromise. They know if their children are exposed to the full range of outside influences that most public schools include, it will weaken religious beliefs and ultimately result in large numbers of their young people leaving the Old Order communities. They fear this because not only do they desire to see their children remain physically close to them in the Amish tradition but they also believe that anyone who leaves the Old Order faith faces the danger of losing salvation for eternity.

The above comments describe the Iowa Amish school situation today and are also reflective of Amish developments in other parts of the nation. The Iowa Amish did not, however, secure control over their school without a struggle. Their controversy began in Buchanan County and can be traced to the 1940s. It was not solved without considerable anguish on the part of all involved.

THE BUCHANAN COUNTY SCHOOL CONTROVERSY

During the more than 130 years that the Old Order Amish have lived in Iowa, their history has been a quiet one. They have lived in isolated settings where Amish fathers have farmed small acreages and the children have attended school in one-room country schoolhouses. Since the late 1940s in Buchanan County, however, several changes in the school situation have affected the Plain People. In 1947 the Hazleton Consolidated School District came into being. That same year the Amish resisted consolidation by assuming all costs of operation of two rural schools and hiring certified teachers. Following the merger of the Hazleton and Oelwein school districts in 1962, however, the Amish rejected certified teachers and hired two of their own eighth grade graduates. Local school officials believed that the Amish were violating the state's school laws and sought ways to force them to comply.

The situation reached a climax on November 19, 1965, when local school officials attempted to force Amish children to board a bus and be transported to the public school in Hazleton. The result was a highly emotional encounter as parents protested by falling to their knees and weeping and children scrambled terrified into a nearby cornfield. The scene of the children bolting was splashed on the front page of newspapers all across the country; the general reaction was swift, widespread, and intensely sympathetic toward the Amish. There were several subsequent showdowns; but not until 1967, when the Iowa General Assembly passed a law that exempted the Amish from hiring certified teachers and from compulsory school attendance, was the problem finally settled. The confrontation that took place that brisk November morning was a very emotional and complex issue. To fully understand that event and subsequent non-Amish community feeling, it is necessary to consider not only the background of the school controversy itself but also factors such as the religious makeup of the area, previous community attitudes toward the Old Order, and the background of the Old Order people themselves.

The Buchanan County settlement is concentrated in northwest Buchanan and southwest Fayette counties, stretching for about twelve miles from Fairbank northeast to Oelwein, with the community of Hazleton located in the southern part of the area. The group is composed of about 130 families located in six church districts. Of the three major Old Order communities in Iowa, Buchanan County is the only one that appears to be static in terms of population. According to a local bishop there has been some out-migration since the mid 1950s but no in-migration; however, the population has remained steady due to marriages among their own young people. Since the start of the school controversy in 1961 a small trickle of families has continued to leave. Some have moved to Wisconsin, others to Honduras and Paraguay, and some have relocated in Milton. [1]

The Amish community in Buchanan County began in 1914 when several Old Order families left Kalona because in their opinion that settlement had become "too worldly." From the beginning the Buchanan County community was marked by more conservative thinking and behavior. Tractors, for example, were allowed for a time; but when models were developed with higher road speeds, the community decided that none should be used. Their rationale was twofold: the tractors enabled the young men to get to town too quickly and caused them to hurry too much with the fieldwork. [2] The Amish themselves view the Buchanan County group as being most conservative and in some ways even backward. Compared to other communities, the Buchanan settlement does not appear to be as prosperous; many houses and barns are not painted regularly, and some barnyards, in sharp contrast to the Kalona Amish, appear cluttered and unkempt. Moreover, land values are considerably lower than those in the Kalona area.

There has also been some concern among the Kalona and Milton Old Order Amish over the lack of parental authority exercised by some Buchanan County parents. Without adequate discipline, some young people had become unruly, outspoken, and difficult to control in the latter 1960s. One incident that highlighted this problem took place in September 1968 when several Amish youths from the Hazleton area went on an unprecedented vandalizing spree. The young men had attended a Sunday night sing that continued into the early hours of the morning, at which time the destructive acts took place. Traveling to different Amish farms, the boys overturned a wagon of shelled corn and an elevator, broke house and barn windows, killed a dozen chickens, and destroyed a binder and a buggy. Several Amish farmers filed complaints with the Buchanan County sheriff, which led to the youths' arrest. They were later charged with "malicious mischief and trespassing." Nine young men were fined and one received a thirty-day jail sentence. These acts and subsequent rebellious behavior earned a bad name for the Buchanan County settlement. Several Amish families later cited this as a reason for moving from the community. [3]

Some parents will tolerate a few rebellious acts from their offspring prior to baptism, but these incidents are usually minor infractions and are controlled by parents and church officials. Continued disobedience and unruliness, as in Buchanan County, is the cause of much apprehension among the Plain People in other communities. The rumor has persisted that several Buchanan County families have been partially ostracized because they were too lenient with their children, and that they were rejected in their subsequent bid to move to another Iowa Old Order community. Although this type of deviant behavior may be limited to several families within the community, it nevertheless gives a negative connotation to the entire settlement.

Religious considerations are significant in understanding the makeup of a community. The Old Order Amish are Mennonites, and although they themselves claim little if any identification with the larger body, the more liberal Mennonite churches such as the General Conference feel a strong religious tie with the Old Order and look upon them as brothers. Kalona, where there is a positive, even protective, attitude toward the Amish, has six Mennonite churches with a combined membership of 1,387. (This does not include either Beachy or Old Order members, nor does it include a sizable number of Kalona Mennonites who attend church in neighboring communities.)[4] On the other hand, Buchanan County has not a single Mennonite church other than the Old Order. Undoubtedly, the common Anabaptist heritage and shared religious beliefs of the Old Order and the other Mennonite groups constitute one reason for the sympathetic and understanding attitude of the Kalona community; while conversely, the absence of these characteristics aids in understanding the unsympathetic and somewhat negative attitudes of many Buchanan County residents.

Another aspect of the religious issue that has produced hard feelings is the Mennonite belief in nonresistance. Since their beginning in the early sixteenth century, they have refused to fight in any war; and if attacked, they will literally turn the other cheek. In recent times, they have filed as conscientious objectors with their local Selective Service boards. In World War II many served as orderlies in military hospitals and worked on government projects such as dam building. In Hazleton during that period, occasional resentment flared over the fact that Amish boys would not fight for their country, and it became intense when news was received that a local boy had been killed in action. At those times Amish youngsters frequently became verbal scapegoats for the hostile community attitude. Even today comments are made to young Amish boys such as "When are you going into the army, son?" which reflect a continuing resentment over their pacifist beliefs.[5] In contrast the Old Order in the Kalona community have had little if any difficulty over this issue because all Mennonites believe in nonresistance.

Because of these factors there is at best, on the part of the general community in Buchanan County, a tradition of tolerance but not acceptance toward the Amish. One expression of this negative feeling is the use of the term, "hookies." Because the Amish reject buttons and substitute hooks and eyes, this term is frequently used in a derisive way by some Buchanan County residents. In other Iowa Amish communities the term is heard infrequently if at all. Many people from Buchanan County make no pretense of their dislike for the Amish and the fact that they would not be unhappy if the entire community were to move away. A salesman from the Oelwein area once attended a service club meeting in Kalona. When the topic of the Amish came up and was discussed positively by Kalona residents, the salesman responded somewhat huffily, "If you love the Amish so much, you can have the ones from Buchanan County too!"[6] No doubt these negative feelings were intensified with the school problems of the 1960s, but there has been a long-standing tradition of half-hearted tolerance or, at best, an attitude of "live and let live" on the part of many Hazleton area residents toward their Amish neighbors.

SCHOOL REORGANIZATION

In 1947 Hazleton Township voted to consolidate with the Independent School District of Hazleton to form the Hazleton Consolidated School District. Before that, all rural area children had attended one-room, country schools. Following consolidation, the Amish community purchased two rural schoolhouses and began operating them as private schools with certified teachers. From 1947 until 1961 the situation remained unchanged, as the Amish provided their own financial support for the upkeep of the two schools and the teachers' salaries.[7] During that period education presented no serious problems for the Old Order Amish, even though their children were taught by certified teachers. Typically, the teachers were older women who had lived in the community for many years and had little desire to inject any new educational concepts or materials into the curriculum. There was, therefore, no reason for the Amish parents to feel threatened. Moreover, while the teachers were certified, not all had completed four years of college work; therefore, all school boards, including the Amish, could hire them at a lower salary level. While teachers' salaries no doubt varied in the community, these were at a level the Amish felt they could afford.

In 1961 the school situation changed dramatically because of a proposed school merger between Hazleton and Oelwein. For many years local residents had discussed the possibility of a merger, with the high school to be located in the larger community of Oelwein since Hazleton's school was inadequate. Oelwein residents naturally favored this move as it would mean a larger school, broadened curriculum, and wider tax base. Hazleton residents, however, had mixed feelings. Some favored the move since they believed their children would receive a superior education; others, fearing that the loss of the high school would weaken the town's economy, and remembering many years of intense rivalry between the two communities, opposed the change. The issue elicited much bitterness and resentment in Hazleton: neighbors stopped talking to each other, a few residents had rocks hurled through their windows, and some old friends even engaged in fistfights.[8] Nevertheless, area voters successfully petitioned for the referendum, and the vote was set for November 8, 1961.

With charges and countercharges flying among Hazleton residents, the Amish tried hard to stay out of the controversy. One move they did make, however, was to petition the local county school authorities that in the event of the merger between the schools, they be excluded from the jurisdiction of the Oelwein officials. They proposed that they be attached to the Fairbank Township area, which still provided one-room schools for the Amish families who lived there. This proposal was rejected, mainly because of objections from Oelwein school officials.[9] This was later justified on the basis that it would have been impossible for the Amish to join the Fairbank district because it involved the crossing of county lines. It is interesting to note, however, that the proposed merger between Hazleton (Buchanan County) and Oelwein (Fayette County) school districts also involved crossing county lines.[10]

Under the existing regulations both school districts had to approve the proposed merger. This presented no problem in Oelwein because there the citizens solidly backed the issue, but in Hazleton the community appeared split about fifty-fifty. Seeking some way to secure a favorable vote in both communities, the Oelwein school superintendent, A. A. Kaskadden, appealed to State Superintendent Paul Johnston for assistance. Johnston suggested that in the event the merger was approved Kaskadden should consider reinstituting one-room elementary schools in the Amish areas. This procedure could be carried out in the following way: the board would incorporate the two schools into the public school system by leasing the buildings, providing certified teachers, and modifying the curriculum to suit the

Amish leaders.[11]   Kaskadden in turn took Johnston's letter to local Amish leader Dan Borntrager to seek support for the proposed merger. Kaskadden pledged his personal backing of Johnston's suggestion that the two Amish schools be reestablished, adding that he expected to be superintendent for a long time and would always "recommend that the board honor our arrangement." The Amish agreed to support the proposal in return for this pledge, apparently believing that the superintendent would support their bid for separate one-room schools, and thus the passage of the merger was assured.[12]

The Amish, knowingly or unknowingly, held the balance of power in the election. Both sides coveted the Old Order vote, but the group opposed to the merger was not concerned because traditionally the Amish did not use their voting privilege; therefore, there was no reason to believe they would do so in the upcoming school election. On November 8, 1961, the school reorganization issue was approved with the Amish participating. The Hazleton vote was a close 264 votes in favor to 215 votes against. Obviously the Amish votes had been decisive, and the antimerger faction was highly incensed to think that the Amish had taken part in the election. Regardless of earlier feelings, Hazleton residents then vowed that the Amish would pay for their part in the affair. Previously, many had "looked the other way" when the Amish cut a few corners in compliance with school laws, such as closing their schools a few days early in the spring. Now, antagonized by Amish action, many area residents declared there would be no more evasion of the law by the Plain People. In addition, they would exert pressure to prevent the newly elected school board from taking over the two Amish schools as promised earlier by Superintendent Kaskadden.[13]

Several months later the Oelwein school board made a number of changes in the original agreement worked out between Kaskadden and the Amish leaders. They informed the Amish that any arrangement to include their schools in the district and thus pay the teachers' salaries could only be temporary. Also, there could be little, if any, "tailoring" of subject matter to comply with religious beliefs of the Amish. The Amish, claiming that these conditions had not been mentioned before the reorganization referendum, believed they had been deceived.

One week later on May 14, 1962, the Amish were again surprised with another apparent reversal in the school board's original commitment to them, when two regional consultants from the state Department of Public Instruction appeared to evaluate their schools. Ostensibly the consultants were to observe the two one-room schools and then advise both the board and the Amish leaders as to what changes must be made before they could come under jurisdiction of the school board as public buildings. The consultants stated that they were "shocked" with conditions, which were much worse than they had imagined. They pointed out the badly worn texts and workbooks and the lack of supplementary reading materials and announced publicly that the schools were in such a deplorable condition they could not possibly be brought up to the standard. Therefore, the state Department of Public Instruction stated that they intended to allow the Oelwein school board to operate the Amish schools for only a limited time—two years at the most—and that the Amish must send their seventh and eighth grade students to the Hazleton Attendance Center. As critics of the policy pointed out at the time, this decision was puzzling and inconsistent since the Fairbank School District was then operating seven one-room rural schools and one two-room rural school for the Amish. Several years later five of these same Fairbank schools were visited by a state official who expressed his approval of the manner in which the district was handling the matter of Amish education.[14] It appeared that there was indeed a double standard for the two districts.

The next move in the growing struggle was made by the Amish themselves. In September 1962 the Amish opened their two one-room rural schools without certified teachers. Contrary to the law, they hired two of their own members, young women with eighth grade educations. Hazleton residents and school officials reacted with surprise, but immediately the feeling surfaced that the Amish had defied the law and must be punished. The question at hand, however, was who should initiate the legal action. After several weeks of discussion among the county attorneys, school board officials, and the county superintendent of schools as well as frequent meetings of the Oelwein School Board, the community received another blow. On the evening of September 25 Superintendent Kaskadden died suddenly. At an emergency meeting the next morning, officials appointed Arthur Sensor as acting school superintendent.[15]

Along with the legal problems posed by the Amish action and the seeming inability of any group to initiate the proper response, one question discussed by all non-Amish groups was, Why? Why did the Amish, after fifteen years of operating their schools with certified teachers suddenly decide to defy the law and hire their own eighth grade graduates?

The general feeling of Hazleton area residents and school officials was that the Amish had taken that position for economic reasons. Dan Borntrager, head of the committee that supervised the two Amish schools and community spokesman, stated on several occasions that teachers' salaries were too high and the Amish could not afford to pay outside teachers, thus substantiating local opinion. At the same time he added that the Amish had no objection to outside teachers except for the cost. He noted that their teachers were paid $120 a month, and he felt an outsider would cost twice that amount. Yet at the same time this was never given as the sole reason. Borntrager continually raised objections to Amish children being taken into Hazleton on the grounds that it violated their religious beliefs. At one point Borntrager commented that "It isn't what they teach in the town school that we object to. It's what they don't teach."[16]

Many Hazleton residents had difficulty viewing the Amish school action as anything but economic in nature since Borntrager was not a religious official but derived power from his economic position in the community. The belief was widespread that Borntrager owned several farms, which he rented to younger Amishmen, as well as having loaned money to several of his people. Thus if he chose to take a stand on the school situation, the others in the Amish community would follow along or remain silent.[17]

FIRST LEGAL ACTION

Legal action was finally initiated by J. J. Jorgensen, Buchanan County superintendent of schools, who filed information with County Attorney William O'Connell concerning the illegal behavior of the Amish school leaders. Before a local justice of the peace on October 20, 1962, nine Amish fathers were charged with sending their children to an unapproved school. Each pleaded innocent and were free on bonds of $25. On November 24 eight went to jail for three days rather than pay fines of $18.50, while one chose to pay the fine.[18]

The Oelwein School Board again attempted to reach a compromise with the Amish by offering another suggestion. Arthur Sensor met with Dan Borntrager on January 2, 1963, with the proposal that if the Amish would agree to send their seventh and eighth grade students to Hazleton immediately, the school board would pay the cost of hiring teachers for the two rural Amish schools. Also attached was the provision that within two years, *all* Amish children would attend school in Hazleton. Sensor further agreed that they would set aside for Amish use a two-room quonset that had previously been used for kindergarten and first grade classes so students would maintain some separation from the other youngsters. Borntrager refused for two reasons: he did not want the Amish children exposed to the outside world as they would be if they attended town school, and he wanted no part of the "two-year" provision.[19]

At this point the Amish initiated legal action when William Sindlinger, a Cedar Falls attorney, volunteered his services. In district court Sindlinger attempted to have his clients exempted from hiring certified teachers on the ground that it interfered with their freedom of religion. On October 28, 1963, District Judge George Heath ruled that Amish children could not be exempt from such requirements. Sindlinger then appealed the case to the Iowa Supreme Court but withdrew before the court issued a decision.[20]

In the meantime, the long-drawn-out controversy had received frequent publicity in newspapers throughout the country, and money from sympathetic readers began to flow into the Amish community. Continual reporting of the situation in the *Budget* also brought money into the settlement, this time from other Amish people. Such events naturally stiffened the backbone of Hazleton residents who already felt they had been deeply misunderstood and even maligned by outsiders who did not understand the situation. Further, they believed that local school officials had made many efforts to meet the Amish more than halfway, and whatever patience they may have had in the initial stages of the controversy had totally dissipated.[21]

THE FINAL SHOWDOWN

In the fall of 1965 events moved rapidly to a climax. First was the election of a new county attorney, Harlan Lemon, who had won much support because of his pledges to get action on the Amish situation and to carry out the laws of the state of Iowa. Also taking office for the first time were four new members of the seven-man Oelwein School Board. The same month the Amish opened their schools for a fourth straight year with noncertified teachers. Reacting to mounting criticism from local residents for inaction, the Oelwein School Board on September 9 began filing charges against Amish parents for failure to send their children to schools with certified teachers. What ensued was again perhaps more than local residents and school officials had anticipated.

The justice of the peace handling the Amish case was Mrs. Minnie Wengert who held court on the front porch of her home in Hazleton. For more than three weeks the Amishmen (sometimes bringing along a gift of garden produce for Mrs. Wengert) appeared nightly, Monday through Friday. At 7:30 each evening school officials testified that Amish fathers had refused to obey the law; each then acknowledged the charge, and fines of $20 plus $4 costs were assessed. They then refused to pay on religious grounds. Although not one of the defendants, Dan Borntrager occasionally attended and quoted a few verses of scripture. He looked every bit the part of a biblical patriarch, unrelenting and steadfast in the face of opposition. In many ways the evening sessions took on a folksy, homespun quality and the press was not to ignore that fact. The following is an excerpt from an account carried by the Des Moines *Register:*

> . . . In Mrs. Wengert's house the other members of the cast are assembled. There's Mrs. Wengert, fussing over the coffee pot and setting out some cookies.
>
> Her husband, Tony, a deputy sheriff is there. So is Sheriff Fred Beier. County Attorney Harlan Lemon, the prosecutor in the case, has a sore back this night and as he awaits the opening of court he is under a heat lamp there in the kitchen.
>
> Amish farmer William E. Borntrager, who is the laughing member of this Amish cast, is there too. He is sipping coffee and reading some file material on the case.
>
> Everyone likes Willie, that's what they call him. Mrs. Wengert is kidding him now about holding the paper too close. "You better get your eyes checked," she smiles.
>
> Mrs. Wengert goes out to the porch and opens the door. "It's chilly out there tonight, don't you fellows want to come in and sit down?"
>
> Amish men, led by their leader Dan Borntrager, file in. Each says, "good evening."
>
> Then the trials begin. Mrs. Wengert sits at the table with the docket book in front of her. Lemon sits to her left, a yellow legal pad on his lap. Sensor sits across from Lemon, his school file open on his lap. The Amish defendant sits to Sensor's right. . . .
>
> Mrs. Wengert asks if the Amish man has anything to say. No. The court finds him guilty. "The fine will be $20 plus $4 court costs," says Mrs. Wengert. "Bond is $40. What do you want to do about the fine?" "The usual," says the Amish defendant. . . .
>
> All of this goes on in a friendly, homely atmosphere. By the time the fifth defendant has appeared Lemon is observed drawing portraits on his legal paper. One has a beard. . . .
>
> Mrs. Wengert gets up once to check the coffee, another time to turn off a dripping faucet in the kitchen. The Amish

men continue to take the defendant's chair. Finally it is the turn of William Bortrager, the amusing Willie of the Amish group.

There is some small talk and finally Sensor says, "I thought you were an old order Amish."

"I only look like one," says Willie. At this his face lights in a grin, then a chuckle, then a belly laugh. The whole room joins in. Willie is so tickled at the turn of events he reaches over and slaps Sensor on the leg. . . . [22]

As the nightly sessions wore on, school and local government officials became increasingly concerned. The Amish did not appear to be weakening in their opposition; if they continued in refusal to pay the fines, their property would eventually be confiscated. It would not take long to ruin the Amish community economically, and the political repercussions of that alternative were so explosive that no one even wanted to consider it!

At this point another move was made by County Attorney Lemon to find a solution. He contacted several Amishmen who did not share Borntrager's strong convictions on the school issue. These people finally agreed that the best face-saving solution for all concerned would be for the Amish children to be taken to the Hazleton school in compliance with Iowa's truancy law. The Amish fathers involved in this plan worked with their people, trying to prepare them for the event. The reasoning was that the Amish, who reject any violent behavior, would certainly express disapproval; but the children, nevertheless, would be moved and after a few days a pattern would be established and everything would run smoothly. Lemon announced to the Amish fathers on the evening of November 18 that the plan would begin the next morning. They were cautioned to explain the procedure to their children to eliminate any confusion when the actual pickup took place. [23]

The following morning an Oelwein school bus headed for the settlement and began making the rounds of the Amish homes. At each farmstead the same situation was discovered: the children were either not there or the father refused to allow them to go with the bus. Finally, the school authorities went to Amish School Number 1 where many children were assembling for the day's session; several parents were also present. The truant officer entered the school and explained the situation to the children. He said that they would receive a warm welcome in Hazleton and asked that they come along quietly and get on the bus. As the children began to file out of the schoolhouse, either the teacher or one of the mothers shouted out in German, ''Run!'' The children ran toward a fence in back of the schoolhouse and then, climbing through or over, scattered through the cornfield into the woods beyond. Some did not stop running until they reached their homes. In the face of the extreme emotional reaction, the school authorities said they would do nothing further that day and returned to Oelwein. Apparently experiencing a change of heart, however, they reappeared in the afternoon and picked up twenty-eight students. Without the presence of their parents, the children were transported peacefully.[24]

The following Monday morning when officials returned to bus the Amish children to town, they met resistance—first by fathers who had blocked the driveway, and then, once inside the school, by praying, weeping mothers on their knees and by frightened children singing ''Jesus Loves Me.'' Dan Borntrager's presence was also recorded, standing with Bible in hand. The scene was later described as one of ''utter bedlam'' as mothers reached protectively for their children and fathers stood up, determined to show their profound opposition to having them taken away on the bus. The school officials, realizing there was absolutely no way to cope successfully with the emotional children and parents, retreated once again. Later that morning Superintendent Sensor, Sheriff Beier, and County Attorney Lemon flew to Des Moines to confer with state officials. The showdown had totally frustrated and incapacitated the beleaguered school men and had left the Amish community in a complete state of shock and disarray. Reporters present on both Friday and Monday, quickly filed their stories, and again the situation received national coverage.[25]

Once in Des Moines, the Oelwein officials conferred with members of the state Department of Public Instruction and Governor Harold Hughes. After the meeting with Hughes it was decided that a three-week moratorium should be enforced to provide a ''cooling off'' period in which a solution possibly could be worked out.[26]

In Buchanan County, officials began making arrangements for a public auction where Amish property would be sold to cover the fines for twenty-four days of missed school attendance. The sale was never held, however, because at the last moment an anonymous donor contributed $1511. The following January two businessmen from Independence, a community eleven miles south of Hazleton, donated $282 to prevent another auction. One sale was actually held, however, where 980 bushels of corn were sold, but Governor Hughes then remitted over $8,000 of the fines. Local leaders, although no doubt relieved that state officials were helping to find a solution to the difficult

"Let's skip the Viet Cong for a moment—what are we gonna do about the Amish school kids in Iowa?"

Reprinted by permission of Newspaper Enterprise Association

school problem, complained that "the governor made asses out of us. We went to court every night for all those weeks, and nothing ever came of it."[27]

Although the intervention by Governor Hughes was perhaps inevitable, it was a move resented deeply by the Hazleton area residents. They were convinced that they were merely trying to enforce the Iowa school laws and were receiving little assistance from state authorities who should have been supportive. Not only was Hughes's original intervention resented but also the subsequent legislation that permitted the Amish parents to hire noncertified teachers. Some residents took the position that the legislation simply "got Hughes off the hook."[28] The governor was caught in an extremely delicate position. As the leading public official in the state, he was charged with upholding state laws; yet he was touched, as were hundreds of others, by the honest pleas of the Amish parents simply to raise and educate their children in their own way. Moreover, Hughes as a political figure could hardly ignore the political repercussions if charges were pressed with repetitions of the earlier, highly emotional confrontations.

THE FINAL SOLUTION

On January 10, 1966, a partial solution was reached. The Amish agreed to lease their schools to the public school district for $1 a year, and the school board agreed to hire certified teachers whose salaries were to be paid by private funds. Other provisions included curriculum adjustments so that no science would be taught, a promise not to use teaching aids such as movie projectors, permission to allow the Amish children to receive two hours per week of instruction in the German language, and a promise by the Amish not to teach religion for the time being. It was later announced on February 22 that the Danforth Foundation of St. Louis had agreed to provide $15,000 to handle the teachers' salaries for the remainder of that school year and the next. Governor Hughes expressed confidence that the 1967 legislature would pass a bill to create a fund for groups like the Amish who desired to have their own schools.[29]

With the opening of the 1967 Iowa legislature, Governor Hughes recommended allocation of a special fund for the hiring of Amish teachers. He specifically asked the following: "Emergency aid for schools, including $50,000 (a year) for aid to school districts in providing certified teachers and other assistance for special rural schools, such schools not having certified teachers at the beginning of the 1965-1966 school year."[30]

When the legislature failed to approve his suggestion, the governor appointed a committee to study the problem. After examining several proposals, the group favored one recommended by the American Civil Liberties Union and asked that the state superintendent of public instruction, with the approval of the Board of Public Instruction, be given the power to "exempt from the school standards those members or representatives of a local congregation of a recognized church or religious denomination established for 10 years or more within the state of Iowa prior to July 1, 1967, which professes principles or tenets that differ substantially from the objectives, goals or philosophy of education embodied in the state-standard law."[31]

A bill embodying that proposal was introduced and after some debate was passed by both the Senate and the House.[32] The original 1967 exemption covered two years and then if the Amish wished to again apply for renewal, achievement tests would be administered to Amish children. If their scores were adequate, the superintendent of public instruction with the approval of the state board could grant another year's exemption.

The passage of this legislation solved the school problem in Buchanan County, but certainly many scars remain. Relationships between the Amish and the non-Amish, never in total harmony, are now perhaps best described as civil. Some non-Amish people feel that resentment against the Amish still surfaces from time to time in the manner in which public services are provided; at times Amish roads are ignored by county maintainers, bridges go unrepaired, and mail is delivered carelessly. It is the feeling of many county residents, however, that the problem may simply disappear in time as more and more Amish families continue to move away. It is doubtful, however, given the emotional experiences of all parties involved, that the school issue will ever be raised again in that area.

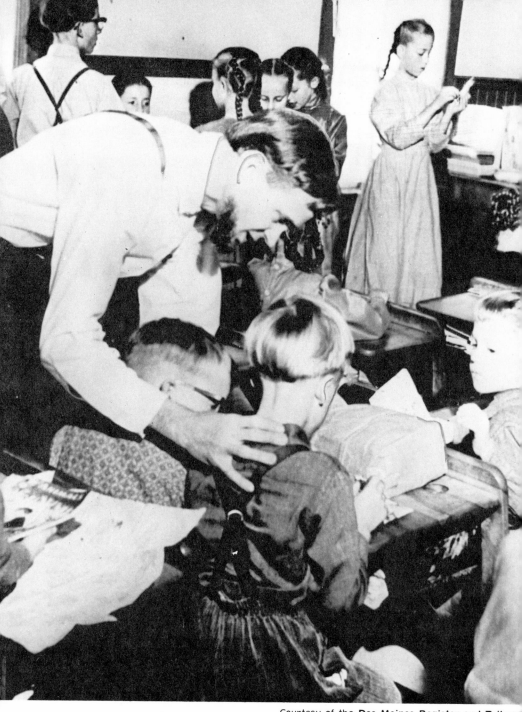

RECESS AT SCHOOL.

The Vital Issue: Education

The settlement reached in the Buchanan County school controversy in 1967 paved the way for other Iowa Amish communities to establish their own schools. Since that time the number has increased gradually until in the spring of 1974, there were sixteen schools maintained by the Old Order and Beachy Amish in the state. A year-by-year exemption has been granted by the state Board of Public Instruction, contingent upon the scores received by the children on the Iowa Tests of Basic Skills and the continued cooperation of the Amish. Even with these solutions, however, problems and misunderstandings have arisen from time to time. The Amish people have indicated a willingness to cooperate and remain open to all suggestions made by state personnel regarding the upgrading of teaching methods and school maintenance.

PRESENT AMISH SCHOOLS IN IOWA

The Old Order Amish community in Kalona did not begin to establish their own schools until after the state legislature passed the law in 1967 that allowed them exemption from hiring certified teachers. In 1968 they established their first parochial school and since then have gradually increased the number. The Kalona change, like Buchanan County, coincided with school reorganization, as the Mid-Prairie School District was formed that year incorporating the Kalona, Wellman, and West Chester districts. The Kalona Old Order Amish, maintaining

113

cordial relations with the general community, have experienced none of the hostile opposition felt so keenly by their Buchanan County brethren. Mid-Prairie District school officials are aware of Amish attitudes and are sympathetic. A short time after the original exemption, the Kalona Beachy Amish congregation also established a private school which they continue to operate.[1]

When the Old Order Amish began a new settlement at Milton in March 1968, they established a private school immediately so there was no need for their children to attend the public school. The following year they added a second school and during the 1974-1975 school term, operated four private schools in the Milton-Pulaski area. The small Old Order group settling west of Bloomfield also established a private school immediately after their settlement in the spring of 1971. The first school there was held in the basement of the Henry Yutz home with eleven Amish children attending. Within a short time, however, they had prepared a separate school building. When a new church district is formed, a new school district usually will be organized within a short time, since the boundaries generally conform.[2]

In April 1974 the state Board of Public Instruction granted to the Beachy Amish congregation at Leon the same exemptions previously allowed other Amish groups. The board's action cleared the way for the Leon group to begin their private school, the Franklin Christian Day School, for the 1974-1975 school term. The Leon Beachy school, which included thirty-six children, was the seventeenth exempt school and brought the total of Amish children attending private schools to 412.[3]

AMISH EXEMPTION

The Amish school bill enacted into law (see Appendix A) during the 1967 session of the Iowa legislature allowed the Amish exemptions in two areas: the first was exemption from the state law that school children attend classes for at least twenty-four consecutive weeks each year until they reach the age of sixteen, and the second was exemption from the requirement that schools employ teachers certified by the state as qualified. The practical meaning is that Amish children are required to attend school only through the eighth grade and that Amish school boards are allowed to hire members of their faith as teachers, most of whom have no education beyond the eighth grade. The first exemption was for a two-year period, and subsequent exemptions have been for one year. The procedure established was for a state Department of Public Instruction consultant to visit each Amish school annually, observe teaching methods, examine teaching materials, and confer with the teacher and school board members. The consultant was to make recommendations to the teachers where appropriate and where it was felt that methods or any other matter needed attention. The state official would then make an annual report to the superintendent of public instruction and recommend whether the Amish should be granted another year's exemption. Also taken into consideration in the final decision were scores on the Iowa Tests of Basic Skills. The superintendent in turn would present the report to the state Board of Public Instruction, composed of lay people appointed by the governor, who would then vote on granting the exemptions.[4]

Since their involvement in the Amish school matter, the board has voted to grant the exemptions for all but one year. In 1971, in a highly surprising move, the board voted not to grant an exemption for the 1971-1972 school year. The negative vote apparently stemmed from the feeling that the Amish schools in Buchanan County were below average and needed considerable improvement before the board would allow their continuation. The decision was made at a July 15 board meeting, which left little time to implement changes since Amish schools were scheduled to begin classes in late August. The negative vote produced great consternation in the Amish communities, and they turned to Governor Robert Ray to intervene on their behalf. After several trips to Des Moines to confer with the governor and officials in the Department of Public Instruction, the Amish invited Governor Ray to visit the Kalona community. There, they declared, he could observe firsthand how the Amish lived and conducted their schools.

Governor Ray accepted and on August 12 he and Mrs. Ray flew to Kalona where they visited an Amish home and two schools. Amishman Tobias Miller, known to everyone as Toby, hosted the noon meal for the governor's party and other guests. Included in the group were local school officials from the Mid-Prairie School District, Amishmen from Milton, and several local residents. The authors also had the privilege of being invited by the Amish to be present for the governor's visit. Since there were many people to feed, Toby and his wife Ruth divided the guests into two groups; the Amishmen from Milton ate at twelve o'clock and then left for the school that Governor Ray would visit early in the afternoon. The second group was to gather at one o'clock. When the governor's party arrived, Toby stepped to the door and, with a twinkle in his eye and a broad warm smile, greeted the governor with ''Good afternoon, Governor. You're just in time for leftovers!'' The dinner served was anything but leftovers as the table fairly sagged with several kinds of meat, vegetables, potatoes, fresh fruits, homemade rolls, and marvelous lemon meringue pie!

Following the meal, everyone drove to the one-room schoolhouse where everything was in readiness for the governor's visit. Even though school was not in regular session, the Amish teacher had gathered the children, and they were all seated at their desks ready for the special visitors. Governor Ray greeted each Amish person individually, including the twenty or more pupils. The children responded with two songs; the first was of a religious nature, but the second told about people and their activities in all Iowa's counties (including something on all ninety-nine!), a song obviously intended to show the governor they had learned many things about their state. A serious discussion followed in which Governor Ray made it clear that his chief concern was whether the Amish would work to provide the best education possible for their youngsters. The Amish, represented by Kalona attorney Lawrence Griffiths, assured the governor that within their religious beliefs, they would do everything they could to upgrade teaching instruction, purchase new textbooks and workbooks, and remain open to suggestions made by state personnel.

The next stop on the governor's agenda was the Beachy Amish school. While there, he asked essentially the same questions of the fathers and teachers and received promises of cooperation regarding a continued effort to improve materials and teaching methods. Later that afternoon after the governor had made a public appearance at the Kalona Sales Barn and was leaving the small community, there was little doubt in anyone's mind that the Amish had succeeded in their attempt to plead their case before the state's highest official. The governor had come to the Amish community, obviously in a sympathetic mood, and like most observers that day he had been visibly touched by what he saw and heard. When the Board of Public Instruction met later that month on the same day that classes began in the Amish schools, they overturned their original vote and granted the exemptions.[5]

Since its inception in 1967 this school arrangement has apparently worked well. At a board meeting in May 1973, Mrs. Edith Munro, a Department of Public Instruction consultant who had worked with the Amish for the previous four years, reported, "Amish-Mennonite schools reflect a continuing effort to improve," adding that the Amish teachers have "asked for and received suggestions in a positive manner."[6] Many important changes have stemmed from the consultant's suggestions, such as monthly meetings between local Amish teachers making it possible for them to discuss mutual problems and concerns. Teachers in the Buchanan County community were advised to visit those in the Kalona area so they could observe more experienced teachers and thus help themselves upgrade materials and methods. In addition, a statewide meeting of Amish teachers takes place periodically so all have an opportunity to interact. In Kalona the school leaders have also established special facilities for children with disabilities such as hearing losses. All children were encouraged to do more reading, and appropriate books were suggested. In the spring of 1974 Mrs. Munro stated in an interview that she believed the program was working successfully and that the Amish had responded cheerfully and positively to her suggestions over the four-year period.[7]

AMISH TEACHERS AND CLASSROOM PROCEDURE

It is stated frequently that the Amish hire their own eighth grade graduates to teach their schools, and the implication is that the teachers have had no training beyond that level. In some ways this is misleading. Many Amish teachers take correspondence courses at the high school level and sometimes at the college level. They are traditionally very conscientious about their responsibilities and utilize every means to inform themselves in areas where they feel it will benefit themselves and their students. A national teachers' publication is issued monthly entitled *The Blackboard Bulletin*, which includes articles of interest and also allows teachers in Iowa to keep up with activities in other states. Local and state meetings are also helpful in this respect.

Perhaps the greatest way, however, that Amish teachers receive training is through apprenticeship. In many areas girls around fifteen and sixteen years of age are hired as teachers' aides. They help keep order in the classroom, assist the children in their work, and help grade routine assignments. After working under an experienced teacher until the age of eighteen, the Amish girl may be hired for a teaching position.

Within the classroom the teacher is expected to maintain firm control. Discipline is regarded as essential if children are going to learn properly. One Amishman in commenting about the good teacher that his school had hired, first cited the fact that she had "good discipline." He then added, "In our schools we teach the four R's rather than the three R's: arithmetic, reading, writing, *and* respect." Criticism by Amish parents about public school education often revolved around the fact that their children could do whatever they wanted, the implication being that the teacher either did not care or was not able to enforce discipline. One Amish father commented that every time he drove past the school his children attended, everyone would run to the window and look out. He was certain that the teacher (who was not Amish but was certified) had little control and, further, probably did not care what the children were doing. He subsequently moved to a different community where the schools were taught by an Amish woman, and he felt his children were learning much more.[8]

Going hand in hand with the role of disciplinarian, is the fact that the teacher also is the symbol of authority. Amish children are taught to respect adults, and in the classroom this is an obvious attitude. Because there is close contact between teachers and parents, Amish children know that any infraction of the rules will be reported quickly to their parents as well as others in the church district. The matter of authority and respect highlights a conflict that the Amish often have experienced when certified teachers from outside communities were hired in their schools. If the teacher was older and somewhat matronly, the conflict was usually minimal; but if the teacher was a young woman, many problems often ensued. Often the young teacher had more progressive ideas on sex education and the study of the human body and would introduce more worldly topics into the Amish classroom. Moreover, she dressed in a fashionable manner with a short skirt, cut her hair, and wore makeup as well as jewelry. Everything about the teacher, although perfectly acceptable by non-Amish standards, violated the religious beliefs of the Plain People. The Amish child, taught from the earliest age to respect and obey all adults including the teacher, experienced a situation of emotional conflict. The teacher was to be respected; yet how could anyone living in such a worldly manner not be sinful? The teacher was to serve as an example of good moral living; yet how could anyone who violated so many religious tenets be respected and obeyed? This was a problem solved only with the hiring of Amish teachers.[9]

Amish parents want the eight years of education their children receive to be as thorough as possible and of the highest possible quality within the confines of their religious beliefs. Parents understand that certain basic skills such as arithmetic, reading, spelling, and language are essential to the proper functioning of their people within Amish society. The Amish feel that any physical education classes are totally unnecessary; many of their children walk or ride horses to school and both before and after school they spend several hours performing chores around the farm. They believe these functions provide ample exercise. Also missing from the school curriculum are any music or art courses, which to the Amish represent "frills." Science courses are tailored to exclude any materials on evolution and human anatomy. The Amish believe that sex education belongs in the home and adamantly oppose any introduction of this into the school curriculum. Each week an Amish father, usually a minister or bishop, visits the school and presents an hour or more of religious education that includes religious beliefs as well as the history of the Amish. Sometimes he also teaches weekly lessons in the German language. Amish youngsters speak only German until they begin school at the age of six, and then they begin to learn English.[10]

The Amish teacher places great stress on developing skills. Amish children take penmanship courses and practice consistently on their letters. Classic arithmetic is taught rather than the new math, and much emphasis is placed on drill in addition and subtraction plus the recitation of the multiplication tables. Workbooks are used in all areas that reflect the emphasis on developing skills. Spelling is a particularly favorite subject, and much like pioneer schools the students have numerous spelling bees. In some Amish communities in the southern states, spelling bees are still held as a form of community entertainment. Each child is taught to complete the tasks begun, and to do them slowly so they will be done well. To hurry through something in a slipshod manner is not consistent with Amish education. This particular attitude has caused problems when taking achievement tests because an Amish child would never skip over a question that was too difficult and go on to the next. Rather, the child would spend as much time as necessary to solve the difficult problem. Obviously, in a timed examination this would be highly detrimental in terms of the final score.[11]

One advantage the Amish have in their self-contained classroom is that the older children are always present and eager to help younger ones with assignments. Educators have been giving considerable attention to this technique, and many believe it is doubly beneficial because both the younger and older student learn better. Not only does the younger child receive individual attention but the older student reinforces learning as well.[12] Unlike most non-Amish children raised in households with only one or two siblings, the Amish have been taught from an early age to assist their many brothers and sisters. In this process they have learned to be concerned about each family member, and the continuation of this attitude in the classroom is both natural and highly beneficial to all concerned.

Most Amish school facilities throughout the state are well-kept, attractive buildings that meet the health standards established by the state Department of Public Instruction. In many cases the Amish have built new schools when they needed to expand. They have been striving to modernize their textbooks and have been gradually replacing old workbooks and texts with new editions. Amish children are happy, wanted, and loved by their parents and their society, and in the classroom this sense of contentment and well-being is apparent. They are serious-minded students who have developed good work habits, and there is seldom any evidence of boredom or disinterest.[13] The children enjoy drawing, and their colorful pictures adorn the walls of the school. With enthusiastic, committed teachers and bright, cheerful classrooms the Amish schools radiate an aura of serious study as well as a feeling of friendliness and well-being.

On the other hand, for those who believe that elementary teachers should promote imaginative projects and insist that a child's world be expanded and the intellect challenged, the Amish schools would be sorely disappointing. Since emphasis is on the development of skills in the basic subjects, memorization and recitation are the order of the day.

VOCATIONAL TRAINING

Much of the criticism leveled at the Amish for their educational philosophies and policies centers around the view that their children are not receiving sufficient education to prepare them to function in non-Amish society. The belief exists that since Amish children are being segregated from the world, if they wish to leave their community they will be unable to do so because of their limited education or, if they do leave, they will have an extremely difficult time surviving economically. In a Wisconsin Supreme Court case, the attorney general argued that economic survival of the Amish was a justification for compulsory school attendance. He stated that the Amish youngsters must have adequate schooling (in this case, a high school education) to prevent their becoming unemployed people who might be a burden on society.[14]

Those who advance these arguments apparently have had little or no contact with Amish society. An extremely important part of Amish life is the time between the end of the eighth grade and the time of baptism and marriage. During this period the young men and women undergo a period of intensive vocational training in which they are taught the skills they need to function independently as capable Amish adults. The Amish believe deeply that the place for the youngster of fourteen and above is in the home; the years between fourteen and twenty are crucial for teaching vocational skills as well as continuing religious training. They also believe that these are critical years for emotional and social development and that all youngsters need to be under the firm guidance of their parents. If removed from the Amish home during these years, the child would be both physically and

SCHOOLTIME WAIT.

religiously incapable of assuming an adult role. The Amish believe that work should be enjoyed and that this comes through learning by doing. If learning is derived from a book, the pleasure will be diminished.

The result of vocational training at home is that Amish children learn how to work and to work hard. Young men not only receive superior agricultural training but also develop skills in carpentry, cinder block laying, house moving, and sawmill operation. Non-Amish individuals who reside in Kalona, Oelwein, or Milton are frequently heard to comment about what "hard workers" the Amish are. Many non-Amish farmers hire Amish boys to help with farm work, recognizing that they have been trained properly and will provide "their money's worth." Frequently Amish youths will be taught to drive a tractor or operate other modern equipment, and interviews with their employers indicate that they learn quickly. The Amish boy who leaves his faith carries with him perhaps the best vocational training he could secure anywhere, in any setting. He has learned through his rigorous upbringing to work hard, accept responsibility, and become self-reliant. The chance of his becoming an unemployed, economic burden on society is very slight. The same situation exists for the Amish girl who has learned how to perform almost any type of domestic work. In Old Order communities many girls between the ages of fifteen and eighteen work as store clerks, waitresses, and nursing aids.

Concern is also expressed by some critics that if the children do leave their faith and attempt education beyond the eighth grade, their poor background will so hinder them they will inevitably fail. No studies have been done in this area, so any conclusion must be tentative. However, specific cases in Iowa refute this reasoning. In the fall of 1970 two Old Order Amish brothers, ages sixteen and seventeen, left their home near Cashton, Wisconsin, to attend high school in Oelwein. The family had formerly resided near there, and the boys had returned to live in the home of a non-Amish friend. Both youths received excellent grades; one was a straight A student while working ten hours a week doing janitorial work, and the other earned A and B grades while working forty hours a week outside the classroom. In addition, both boys were taking a correspondence course in German from the University of Nebraska. In a newspaper interview the boys gave ample reasons for wanting to leave the Amish faith, but both supported the excellent work experience they had received. Commented one youth, "I am not sorry I was raised Amish. It taught me to accept responsibility." His brother added, "We were taught to do our work and our best at all times. It was good experience. We know there are worse things than this kind of life."[15] Cases such as this support the findings of nationally known Amish authority John Hostetler who has written that Amish youngsters who desire to seek more education "are generally highly motivated and capable of doing so" and are not disadvantaged educationally. [16]

In some parts of the nation, although not in Iowa, Amish children attend a more formalized vocational school. Vocational classes typically meet on a regular basis and reports are filed by Amish youngsters and their parents regarding the training they receive at home and the work they do in connection with it. The precedent was set in Pennsylvania in 1955 when that state recognized a plan worked out between the Pennsylvania Department of Public Instruction and Amish leaders. The plan, called the "Policy for Operations of Home and Farm Projects in Church-Organized Day Schools," came about after some eighteen years of conflict. Amish youngsters, who have completed the eighth grade but are not old enough to apply for a farm work permit, are permitted to enroll in the vocational school. The school is taught by an Amish person and offers English, mathematics, health, and social studies as well as home projects in agriculture and homemaking. Students perform work at home under the direction of their parents, keep a record of daily activities, and meet in a classroom situation a minimum of three hours each week. Since 1955 the plan has been adopted in other states as well.[17]

Another facet of Amish education that should be considered is the number of young people who actually do leave their faith each year. Again, no specific study has been made in this area, and exact figures would be extremely difficult to obtain since Amish people are naturally reluctant to talk about the matter. One highly respected leader, however, estimated that between 10 and 15 percent of their young people leave the Old Order faith. Given their high birthrate, the Amish appear to be more than holding their own, however. A second consideration is that most who do leave the Old Order do not go very far. The same Amish leader estimated that 95 percent join either Beachy Amish or Conservative Mennonite congregations that embrace similar theological doctrines and beliefs on educational matters, particularly the preference for an eighth grade education.[18]

SUPREME COURT DECISIONS

While the Iowa Amish have never been involved as litigants in a lawsuit that was reviewed by either the Iowa or the United States Supreme Courts, Amish groups in other states have been involved in court disputes. Although this participation has not affected nor does it now directly affect the implementing of Iowa's school laws, it indirectly influences the thinking of public school and state government officials in decisions regarding school exemptions and the Iowa Amish. For this reason it seems appropriate that two major court cases be reviewed briefly.

In 1968 three Amishmen in Wisconsin refused on religious grounds to send their children to high school. In doing so they were breaking a Wisconsin state law requiring all children to attend school until age sixteen. The Amish fathers (two were members of the Old Order and one a member of the Conservative Amish Mennonite Church) were tried and convicted in Circuit Court of Green County for defying the state's compulsory attendance law. The case was appealed, however, and the Wisconsin Supreme Court in *Wisconsin* v. *Yoder,* reversed the convictions, granting the Amish an exemption from attending school beyond the eighth grade. The court based its decision on the grounds that the compulsory school attendance law violated their religious prohibition against formal education. The court observed that the Amish believe secondary schools teach "an unacceptable value system" and that "they also seek to integrate ethnic groups into a homogenized society. . . ." The court further commented that the education the Amish received beyond eighth grade was "irrelevant to their lives" or would make it impossible for them to continue as Amish.[19]

The Wisconsin attorney general then requested a hearing before the United States Supreme Court, which on May 15, 1972, upheld the decision handed down in *Wisconsin* v. *Yoder*. Chief Justice Burger, in delivering the opinion of the Court, pointed out that Amish objection to formal education beyond the eighth grade was firmly grounded in their religious concepts. He stated, "Formal high school education beyond the eighth grade is contrary to Amish beliefs, not only because it places Amish children in an environment hostile to Amish beliefs . . ." but also "takes them away from their community physically and emotionally, during the crucial and formative adolescent period of life."[20] In answer to the charge that Amish children would be ill-equipped for life if they did not have one or two years of schooling beyond the eighth grade, Chief Justice Burger wrote that there is no evidence to show that "upon leaving the Amish community Amish children, with their practical agricultural training and habits of industry and self-reliance, would become burdens on society because of educational shortcoming." Also related was the fact that Amish children receive excellent vocational training. The Court therefore affirmed the decision of the Supreme Court of Wisconsin that the First and Fourteenth Amendments "prevent the State from compelling respondents to cause their children to attend formal high school to age 16."[21]

While not directly affecting the manner in which state officials handled the matter of Amish education in Iowa, these decisions undoubtedly strongly reinforced existing attitudes regarding the correctness of granting Amish school exemptions there.

EXEMPTIVE MEASURES VS. SUPPORTIVE MEASURES

During the years since the Amish received their initial exemption, concern has occasionally been voiced by school officials as well as private citizens that perhaps other religious minorities or special groups might also request the right to hire noncertified teachers. Would other religious groups who provide private schools for their children qualify for the same exemptions if they were to request them?

In December 1973 this question became more than rhetorical. The parents of students who attended the Central Iowa Christian Academy in Marshalltown, a newly opened Baptist elementary school, requested that their children be exempt from the state educational standards law. In effect, the Baptists were requesting the right to hire noncertified teachers. They wrote Superintendent of Public Instruction Robert Benton that they believed their objectives, goals, and philosophy differed in many areas from those practiced in the public schools. These areas were evolution, sex education, humanism, secularism, materialism and temporalism, permissiveness, relativism, and socialism. Superintendent Benton refused the request, stating that he did not believe the Baptists had "presented a bona fide case showing where their basic religious tenets are in conflict with any of the standards set forth by this state board." On the other hand, Benton concluded, the Amish did make such a case. He presented his decision to the state Board of Public Instruction who in turn concurred with his opinion. [22]

While concerns continue to be raised by members of the state school board and others that Amish exemptions might lead to increased requests from other religious groups, this seems unlikely. Even the case of the Marshalltown Baptists supports this contention, as they have been the only group other than the Amish to request consideration. The state Department of Public Instruction allows some latitude in the selection and content of courses taught; for example, local schools are not required to teach the theory of evolution or sex education in their science or biology courses. Because of this flexibility, individual schools can often circumvent subject areas that might be objectionable to them.

In most private schools the chief concern is not attendance laws, teacher certification, or curriculum but is financial. As teachers' salaries have risen, as more extensive materials and complex equipment have been needed, and as special programs like remedial reading have been developed, private parochial school boards are finding it increasingly difficult to provide quality instruction, modern facilities, and broad curriculums for their students. Their chief concern has been, and no doubt will continue to be, the skyrocketing costs and whether they will be able to continue meeting them with monies from their congregations. The Iowa legislature in 1974 passed a bill, H. 1476, that illustrates this point. This requires local school districts to transport private school children in public school buses. To implement the change, the legislature called for the appropriation of $2,200,000 to reimburse local schools for costs and $2,200,000 for transportation equipment needs. The requests of private schools fall into the category of supportive measures that will help lighten their financial loads. The Amish, on the other hand, have an entirely different set of concerns that can only be met by allowing exemptions from certain state imposed regulations, thus placing their requests in the area of exemptive measures.[23]

CONCLUSION

In Iowa the Old Order Amish appear to have worked out their differences with state education officials, and no major problems appear on the horizon. The Amish have accepted constructive criticism in a positive manner and as a result quality of instruction, textbook and workbook materials, and physical facilities have improved considerably. There is no reason to believe that they will not continue to cooperate fully with state officials.

A study of the educational philosophy and practices of the Plain People points out once again, and perhaps even more dramatically than before, the extent of the integration and cohesiveness that exists in their society. Their religious tenets dictate that they live as a "peculiar people," and the only way this is possible is to maintain total control over all their societal institutions. Inherent in their view is the need to isolate themselves from the outside world; live in a rural setting; earn their livelihood as farmers; dress in a plain and humble fashion; and raise their children in a secluded, tightly controlled environment. Any violation of these precepts must be avoided at all costs. If Amish children are forced to attend the public schools with their large attendance centers, extracurricular activities, emphasis on modern living, teaching of sex education, busing schedules, and education beyond the eighth grade, they would daily face countless violations of their religious convictions. Close friendships would be formed with non-Amish youngsters, participation would be demanded in activities viewed as being immoral and worldly, and religious beliefs would undoubtedly be challenged and weakened. Only in an isolated setting, where Amish parents are involved in school planning, with a teacher selected from their midst and a limited curriculum, can the Amish find harmony between what they believe the Bible admonishes them to believe, and how they actually live their lives.

In the opinion of many state education officials as well as Amish leaders, Amish children in Iowa are receiving an eighth grade education that adequately prepares them for their way of life. Unless some unforeseen circumstance arises, it appears that the Amish in Iowa are in the process of achieving a satisfactory solution to their school problems.

Photo by Joan Liffring Zug

BEACHY AMISH MAY OWN
BLACK AUTOMOBILES.

The Beachy Amish

A frequent distinction made between Amish members is whether they are "house Amish" or "church Amish." The terms indicate a basic difference between the Old Order and the Beachy groups, as the Beachy worship in churches and the Old Order conduct religious services in their homes. Adhering to many of the religious beliefs and social customs of the Old Order, the Beachy groups nevertheless deviate in several significant ways. Overall, they are more liberal in their economic practices and less concerned about maintaining separation from the world. Beachy Amish members work in nonfarm related industries, own automobiles (if they are black), and interact on a more frequent basis with non-Amish people.

THE ORIGINS OF THE BEACHY AMISH

The Beachy Fellowship has been in existence since the 1920s when it originated in Somerset County, Pennsylvania.[1] During that decade friction developed in the district of Moses M. Beachy, an Old Order Amish bishop of the Casselman River District. The conflict centered around the use of electricity, the ownership of automobiles, and the practice of holding Sunday school. Eventually, the controversy also involved more fundamental church doctrine when Bishop Beachy refused to excommunicate and shun members of his congregation for joining Conservative Amish Mennonite churches.[2] In 1927 the situation reached a climax when the most conservative members of the involved districts withdrew and joined other Old Order church districts so they would not lose their good standing. This division resulted in the Yoder (Old Order) and the Beachy congregations, both being named after their respective ministers at that time.[3]

During the next three decades other Old Order church districts followed Beachy's example until Beachy congregations were located in many states throughout the central and eastern United States. In 1974 there were Beachy congregations in sixteen states, the District of Columbia, and five foreign countries, with the heaviest concentrations in Pennsylvania and Ohio. Their membership at that time was 4,069 located within sixty-two congregations. Although there are a few exceptions, the great majority of Beachy Amish are either former Old Order members or their descendants. On rare occasions a non-Amish might join the Beachy group or a Beachy member might marry a non-Amish who then joins. Throughout North and South America as well as Iowa the Beachy Amish constitute approximately one-fifth of the total Amish population.[4]

The Iowa Beachy Amish church began near Kalona in 1946. Typical of previous church schisms, disagreement arose among some Johnson County Old Order members over the use of modern equipment. Precipitating the controversy was the fact that Johnson County highway officials had applied an oil surface to roads in the southern part of the county and had then prohibited the use of vehicles with lugs. Members of the North Church District agreed to use rubber on their machinery, but this decision brought an immediate, negative reaction from other districts. Action was taken to prevent the North District from going ahead with adoption of rubber tires, and gradually the question of other modern conveniences and equipment also became involved. Soon members were arguing over the propriety of using electricity, owning automobiles, and installing telephones. The more liberal members began to challenge the traditional arguments with comments like "if it is wrong to own a car or use a telephone then why is it right to hire a car or use a neighbor's phone."[5]

As a result of the bickering, seven families left the Old Order church and began meeting separately for religious services; these Amish fathers were Moses E. Yoder, Willie Helmuth, Enos H. Miller, John Helmuth, Chris Stolzfus, Mose Coblentz, and Benedict Kemp. Their place of worship was an unused Lutheran church located northeast of Kalona at Kesselring Junction. Hard feelings continued, however, as many homes were affected with sons and daughters leaving the Old Order and "going Beachy."[6]

Ministers from Beachy churches in other states came to preach until John Helmuth and Moses E. Yoder were ordained as ministers during the winter of 1946. The Beachy adopted the name, Burkholder Church, after a minister by that name who had visited the group. In 1952 the members built a church five miles north of Kalona and changed their name to Sharon Bethel. From the modest beginnings of seven families, by 1974 the congregation had grown to forty-one families and a membership of ninety-nine.[7]

BEACHY EXPANSION

Beachy groups, like the Old Order, have experienced difficulty in finding available, reasonably priced land, and this problem led them to establish their second Iowa settlement at Leon. In searching for new areas, the Beachy have followed the same pattern utilized by the Old Order. The procedure is for several members to form a search committee and travel to places where they know land is for sale. Not only is price a factor but also the possibility of additional farms coming up for sale in the future. The Beachy committee discovered when they visited the Leon area that many of the farmers were between sixty and seventy years old and were obviously considering retirement. Land values averaged $80 an acre. The two prerequisites of land prices and land quantity were thus satisfied. The first Beachy settlers—the Moses E. Yoder family and the Wayne Miller family—moved to Leon in February 1959. The families that followed in the next few years came from Oklahoma, Kansas, Virginia, Pennsylvania, Indiana, and Oregon and brought the total number of families to twenty-five. During the most recent years the Beachy young people have married within their community, and the number of families in 1974 was thirty with a total membership of eighty.[8]

Seldom, however, is the reason for resettlement totally economic. The feeling exists among the Iowa Beachy that the Leon group is the most liberal and that the members who came to Leon were perhaps a little more progressive than their home congregations would have liked. By moving to a new area where they were involved in shaping the rules of conduct, they could accommodate their more liberal feelings. This avoided confrontation in their home congregation and possibly eliminated any desire to leave the Beachy group for a less strict Mennonite church. As with the Old Order, the ability to migrate without loss of prestige or church rights or privileges provides the Beachy members with a safety valve for their discontent.[9]

The Leon community reacted somewhat negatively when news of the impending Beachy settlement began to circulate. Rumors flowed freely that the Mennonite people were invading southern Iowa with forty families in the initial settlement alone and that they would set up an independent economic organization. They would have their own banks, stores, and other service operations so they would have no need of the services of locally owned businesses. Also heard frequently was the rumor that they planned to purchase all the land and drive non-Amish people from the area. Apparently the Leon residents had mistaken the Amish for the Amana residents located west of Iowa City. They believed that the Amish were going to establish a similar society where the stores, industrial plants, and land were to be owned by a corporation.[10]

Moses E. Yoder began to counteract these allegations by attending the Leon Ministerial Council, which was composed of local ministers. He managed to successfully interpret the Mennonites' religious beliefs and positions as well as their migration plans. The local ministers, in turn, relayed this information to their parishioners. A close relationship developed between Minister Yoder and the Ministerial Council, and no doubt the understanding stemming from this relationship was highly significant in calming many fears about the Mennonite "invasion." Gradually, misapprehensions began to fade and the community observed that the Beachy members were pleasant, hardworking, thrifty people. In fact, many older farmers who were anticipating retirement began to approach Yoder and offer to sell him their farms. It began happening so frequently that Yoder commented, "Everytime some older man drove in, I knew he had a farm to sell."[11]

GENERAL CHARACTERISTICS

The Beachy Amish in Iowa have retained many characteristics of the Old Order, but many areas of contrast continue to exist. Economically, the Beachy are not so concerned about isolating themselves from the outside world. While most Beachy men are farmers, many others seek employment in outside areas. In the Leon congregation some are employed at a ready-mix plant in Davis City and others operate a window factory and a blacksmith shop in Decatur City. Carpentry, mechanical work, and truck driving also attract Beachy wage earners. In the agricultural area, the Beachy use tractors and electrical equipment, undoubtedly saving time and making them less dependent on the manual labor provided by large families. Their acreages remain small, however, so they are still forced to practice extreme frugality in their buying habits, whether the expenditures are for farm equipment or domestic needs. Their machinery is more up-to-date than the Old Order, and many do custom combining throughout their area.[12]

One aspect of their economic activities that presents a conflict for some Beachy members is working in areas where employees are traditionally unionized. While Beachy members recognize that unions have brought about great improvements in working conditions and wages, they still refuse to identify themselves with any group that might resort to force or power. Pointing out that unions sometimes use mob tactics and violence, they resist membership in such organizations and point out instead that the Bible teaches a better way: ". . . all things . . . ye would that men should do to you, do ye even so to them . . ." (Matthew 7:12). "Let all bitterness, and wrath, and anger, and clamour, and evil speaking, be put away from you, with all malice" (Ephesians 4:31). "And the servant of the Lord must not strive; but be gentle unto all men . . ." (II Timothy 2:24). To guide their members in these areas, the Beachy suggest the following:

1. That members seek employment where union membership is not required.
2. That farmers likewise refrain from membership in farmers unions which also thrive on coercive and sometimes destructive methods.
3. That if and when unions do take control, and if employment or market is restricted to union members, a transfer of employment or market is recommended.[13]

The Beachy recommend one further alternative in the area of employment with a unionized company. The agreement or "basis of understanding" is similar to one prepared by a Mennonite general conference on industrial relations and was approved by officials of both the American Federation of Labor and the Congress of Industrial Organization. Under these agreements the Mennonite employees will:

1. Contribute to a specified cause, usually charitable or benevolent, a sum of money equivalent to the amount of dues paid by the union members.
2. Refrain from interference with or resistance to union activities.
3. In case of conflict resulting in a strike or similar action between the union and the employer, maintain an attitude of sincere neutrality.
4. Abide by the regulations of the shop and union with regard to wages, hours, and working conditions (as long as such regulations do not violate biblical principles).[14]

The unions, in turn, agree to excuse the nonresistant employee from membership in the union, payment of union dues, attendance at meetings, and other union activities.[15]

The Beachy have not adhered as strongly to their separationist tendencies in regard to education as have the Old Order. The Kalona Beachy group has their own school, Sharon Bethel, with a 1974 enrollment of seventy students. The school contains three classrooms and hires three teachers. In Leon, however, children attended the public school until September 1974, when they opened their own private school. This action stands in sharp contrast to the Milton-Pulaski Old Order Amish who organized a school almost immediately upon settlement of their families in that area. The Beachy do believe, however, that an eighth grade education is sufficient and that private schools hiring Beachy Amish teachers are the best way to educate their children.[16]

The Beachy provide further religious training for their young people at the Calvary Bible School at Calico Rock, Arkansas. Beachy congregations throughout the nation finance and administer the school, and Beachy ministers teach the courses. As the school's name indicates, it is a Bible school and most courses center around that theme. Also offered, however, are elementary courses in music, typing, and German. Three sessions, each lasting three weeks, are held during January and February. At one time or another most Beachy young people from Kalona and Leon attend the school.[17]

Beachy and Old Order members share common religious convictions. The Beachy believe in nonconformity to the world and nonresistance and accept the *Dortrecht Confession of Faith*. They believe as well in the Christian ordinances of foot washing, head coverings for women, the laying on of hands, holy marriage, and the practice of the holy kiss between Christian believers. The major religious difference is the Beachy use of a separate church building.[18]

Like all Mennonites, the Beachy believe in nonresistance and therefore will not serve in any military capacity. They believe that as Christians it is inconsistent for them to "participate in military service, whether combatant or noncombatant, whether in defense or offense, for Christ has commanded us to love even our enemies." To support their pacifist views, the Beachy quote the biblical verse (Matthew 5:39), which states that in the event of conflict, they should turn the other cheek.[19] They believe their people should take positive action by giving financial aid to the needy and distressed, clothing the naked, and in all ways seeking to overcome evil with good. In the event of all-out war, the Beachy believe that the Scriptures require them to "flee, or suffer the spoiling of our goods, rather than to inflict injury even on an enemy." (See also Matthew 5:40-44, 10:32; Romans 12:19.)[20]

Like the Old Order, the religious convictions of the Beachy prevent them from any involvement in political matters. They believe in separation of church and state and that one has no right to interfere in the activities of the other. The Beachy further believe that since they subscribe to biblical nonresistance they therefore cannot participate in a system that bears the carnal sword, "for the weapons of our warfare are not carnal" (II Corinthians 10:4). The same beliefs prevent them from participating in political campaigns, political rallies, and elections, "for by so doing we would identify ourselves with the system." The Beachy believe that because of God's absolute power over men, they can accomplish more by their prayers than others can by voting against one another at the polls.[21]

THE BEACHY FELLOWSHIP

The Beachy church is considered a fellowship as opposed to a specific conference. Like the Old Order, each congregation is autonomous, with a bishop presiding over the membership and assisted by two ministers. The Beachy believe in a support ministry but not a paid one, which means that if the bishop or ministers find they are behind in their own chores because of church obligations, other members of the congregation will assist with fieldwork, harvesting, or whatever needs to be done. The bishop and ministers are chosen by lot. Once a year church officials attend a general assembly to discuss common problems; Erwin N. Hershberger of Myersdale, Pennsylvania, serves as secretary for the National Assembly. Within each church district the bishop conducts communion and performs baptisms and marriages. The ministers assist him with the preaching and give supportive council. In Kalona the church services are conducted in German, but in Leon English is used. Sunday morning church services are alternated with Sunday school. When Sunday school is held, evening church services are conducted. On the alternating Sunday, the young people have a special meeting. Once a month they also hold a social get-together called a "literary." The entertainment consists of games, singing, and the presentation of a skit written and acted out by members of the group. In addition the young people distribute religious tracts in Iowa City, present religious services and singing at the state penitentiary in Fort Madison, and conduct services at the Sunshine Rescue Mission in Cedar Rapids. Disabled persons and widows within the church are also given special assistance.[22]

The age at which Beachy young people are baptised presents yet another contrast with the Old Order, who believe in adult baptism based on confession of faith. The Beachy do not stress the adult aspect but rely instead on the confession of faith. Many Beachy young people are baptised at age fifteen and sixteen and some as young as twelve and thirteen. One Beachy bishop stated that they feel the time for baptism has arrived when the young person begins looking for something more in his or her life.[23]

The practice of shunning also differs between the two Amish groups. The Beachy will not shun anyone for joining a more liberal Mennonite group, and only under the most extreme conditions will they shun one of their members. They make every effort to work with the wayward one, showing love and concern and aiding in every way possible, hoping that the group behavior will help the individual see ''the true way'' and return with the proper repentance. They interact with all Mennonite church groups from the most conservative such as the Old Order to the more liberal such as the Conservative Mennonites.[24]

Council meetings are held twice a year, several weeks before communion Sunday. The purpose is to review the rules and regulations with the entire congregation. It is a time when wrongdoings can be pointed out to members; if the problems are solved, they can take part in the communion service; if not, however, they do not partake. Overall, the Beachy elders are not as strict as the Old Order regarding their young peoples' behavior. For instance, the Beachy allow their young people to buy tape decks for their automobiles as long as they contain religious music, while they will not allow them to have regular radios. Their rationale is that one can control what the young people listen to on the tapes, but they cannot control what they listen to on the radio.[25]

Needy and disabled persons outside their own church community are also a concern of the Beachy. Membership in the Mennonite Central Committee (MCC), the official relief and service agency for North American Mennonites, provides a means of aiding needy people all over the world. The MCC coordinates and administers programs in the areas of foreign relief and services, voluntary services, mental health, and peace and disaster services. A Beachy Amish member from Pennsylvania sits on the seventeen-man MCC board that meets annually to review programs and determine future outreach. The Leon group contributes regularly to the MCC through periodic meat canning operations. The Beachy cooperate with the Old Order River Brethren, a small group within the Brethren church located at Dallas Center. The two congregations donate animals or money to purchase them, and a mobile unit operated by the MCC comes to Leon where the butchering is done. A health inspector is always present to certify that the process meets federal government standards. The cans of food are then turned over to the MCC for distribution.[26]

The Beachy also have their own separate mission organization, the Amish Mennonite Aid. Founded in 1955, the headquarters are located in East Rochester, Ohio, with the governing board composed of Beachy ministers located throughout the United States. The agency's main emphasis is upon overseas mission work, with most attention directed to British Honduras, El Salvador, and Costa Rica. Missionary work is also being carried out in Germany. The Beachy purpose is stated as follows in their "Overseas Voluntary Service Manual":

1. To help meet physical, spiritual, and emotional needs of individuals which otherwise would not be met.
2. To demonstrate a positive witness which testifies to the love and power of God and to the life of a Christian by helping others to help themselves by providing information, encouragement, love, tools, and materials.
3. To live together as a group in a way that will demonstrate what true Christianity really means.
4. To strengthen the outreach of the church through daily, consistent life, and by easing the sufferings of those less fortunate, thereby demonstrating Christianity in shoe leather; by assisting the work of missions whenever this is jointly agreed upon by those who are responsible. [27]

The group's domestic work consists of sponsoring and operating the old folks home in Harrison, Arkansas, and children's homes at Plain City, Ohio, and Mission Home, Virginia. An additional function of the mission's overseas program is that it provides many young Beachy men with the opportunity to fulfill their Selective Service requirements for military exemptions through voluntary missionary work. [28]

As well as their own missionary group, the Beachy also have an official publication, the *Calvary Messenger*, published by Calvary Publications, Meyersdale, Pennsylvania. Many Beachy families also subscribe to *Family Life,* a magazine published eleven times a year by Pathway Publishers, Aylmer, Ontario. [29]

Perhaps it is in the area of general social behavior that the most noticeable differences appear between the Beachy and the Old Order. Both groups believe in the precept of nonconformity to the world, but the manner in which they enforce it depends upon their interpretation of what is worldly and what is not. This interpretive process apparently affords considerable latitude for the Beachy in determining their social behavior. Beachy members wear more modern clothing, have increased business contacts with non-Amish people, and take part in extension programs, all of which indicate a more liberal interpretation of the nonconforming principle than that made by the Old Order.

The Beachy lack the uniformity of dress that is so much a part of the Old Order. The older men wear the traditional Amish garb of broadfalls trousers and plain colored shirts, but wear shorter beards and have their hair parted in the middle and cut quite short. The women wear a long cape style dress, but often made with bright-colored material. They have dark stockings and a prayer cap that is smaller than in the Old Order. In general, their dress is simply less old-worldish. Beachy young people dress with varying degrees of modernity, as some young men wear regular short-sleeved sport shirts and work-style trousers during the week. However, on Sunday they wear traditional garb. Some young men who do wear the front-drop trousers have abandoned suspenders and started wearing belts. With the emphasis today on longer hair styles and beards, it is difficult to distinguish between many of the Beachy young people and the general non-Amish population.[30]

In their day-to-day activities, Beachy members interact to a high degree with non-Amish people. At different times Beachy members have taken part in short courses offered by county extension officials, such as a tailoring course. In one instance, five foster children were placed in Beachy homes, necessitating continual contact with welfare officials. The involvement of a Beachy minister in the Leon Ministerial Council offers another example of their social relationships with non-Amish people. Overall, this high degree of interaction is apparently regarded positively by both Beachy and non-Beachy Amish groups. On the other end of the spectrum, there appears to be little social interaction with members of the Old Order. While business contacts are maintained between Beachy people in Leon and certain Amish communities such as Jamesport, Missouri, some Beachy members have never visited the Amish community in Buchanan County.[31]

CONCLUSION

The two Beachy congregations in Iowa have grown steadily since their beginnings in 1946 and 1959. Nationwide, the Beachy group is enlarging at an even greater rate; since the 1960s Beachy congregations have multiplied so rapidly that many Iowa members have not been able to remain knowledgeable as to the total number of groups and their locations. They exhibit the same high degree of mobility as their more conservative counterparts, and there is every indication that the Beachy group will increase both in membership and in number of settlements. Within Amish society the crucial question is, How many Old Order members will go Beachy? Undoubtedly they will attract a small percentage, but as they become more modern in their dress, more worldly in their economic habits, and increase their social relationships with non-Amish people, this will increasingly discourage Old Order members from joining their church. The closer the Beachy remain in religious thinking and practice to the Old Order, the more converts they will attract. The trend, however, appears to be in the direction of the Beachy becoming more worldly and thus attracting fewer Old Order members. As they move in that direction, dropping the word Amish from their name and thus becoming the Beachy Mennonites becomes more probable.

⌀ Old Order Amish

◇ Beachy Amish

Arkansas
1. Mountain View

Illinois
1. Arthur
2. Sullivan

Iowa
1. Riceville-McIntire
2. Hazleton
3. Kalona
4. Leon
5. Bloomfield
6. Milton

Kansas
1. Garnett
2. Hutchinson
3. Haven

Minnesota
1. Wadena
2. Grove City
3. Canton

Missouri
1. Jamesport
2. Macon
3. Bowling Green
4. Clark
5. Windsor
6. Fortuna
7. Marshfield
8. Seymour
9. Dogwood
10. Mountain View

Oklahoma
1. Chouteau
2. Thomas

Wisconsin
1. Curtis
2. Spencer
3. Amherst
4. Wilton
5. Cashton
6. Westby

MAP 3. Old Order and Beachy Amish settlements in the north central states.

The Plain People
in the Midwest

Throughout the Midwest, the Old Order Amish are becoming increasingly visible. Many eastern Amish families faced with soaring land prices, particularly in Pennsylvania, are looking to areas like Missouri, southern Iowa, and southern Minnesota where land is available and reasonably priced. A number of Amish families have also moved out of the United States, resettling in Central and South America as well as Canada. Conservative Mennonite church groups have also initiated new settlements in Missouri and these have been expanding rapidly since 1970. Perhaps because of these resettlement practices as well as the restrictive nature of Amish life, the belief persists that large numbers of the young people are leaving their religion and that the Old Order Amish are doomed to eventual extinction. However, a close examination of their communities in the Midwest leads to the inevitable conclusion that the Amish are a rapidly growing, prosperous people who do not in any sense appear to be declining in numbers or conviction.[1] The settlements established since 1950 in Iowa, Missouri, and Minnesota, with a few exceptions, have increased rapidly in population and most appear to be strong, ongoing communities with every prospect of increased future growth. As land prices continue to escalate and population becomes denser in traditional Amish areas such as Lancaster County, Pennsylvania, and Holmes County, Ohio, the midwestern Amish communities in Minnesota, Iowa, and Missouri will no doubt continue to expand in both size and number. Their status as given here reflects 1974 conditions.

MISSOURI OLD ORDER AMISH SETTLEMENTS

Although the first Amish Mennonite church was organized in 1860 near Garden City, Missouri, the present Old Order Amish communities are of more recent origin. Six groups were established in the mid-1900s, and by 1957 the following settlements existed in Missouri: Bowling Green, North; Bowling Green, South; Jamesport; Green Ridge; Clark; and Macon.[2] The Green Ridge Old Order group has since become extinct, and the two Bowling Green communities have merged.

The largest Missouri Old Order community is Jamesport. Beginning in 1953 with five families from Delaware and Iowa, the group has expanded rapidly and contains five church districts with a total of slightly over 100 families.[3] The second largest Missouri settlement is Bowling Green, one of the first Old Order communities in Missouri. The group began in 1948 when five families moved from Berne and Portland, Indiana, and Dover, Delaware. This community includes ninety-four families situated within four church districts.[4] Clark has the third largest Missouri Old Order Amish population and is divided into four church districts. This settlement began in the fall of 1953 with the first families moving from Fairbank, Iowa (Buchanan County), and includes approximately seventy families.[5]

Somewhat smaller in size as well as being of more recent origin are the Old Order communities of Seymour, Macon, and Marshfield. The Old Order Amish started the Seymour community in 1968 when some twenty families moved from Geneva, Indiana. The group has since expanded to include thirty-five families. The Macon community (sometimes referred to as the Anabel settlement because the first families had Anabel addresses) began in the fall of 1956, with families from Taylor County, Wisconsin, along with one family from Buchanan County. Later, families settled there from Arkansas, Indiana, and Wisconsin along with Missouri Amish from Jamesport and Bowling Green. The group has expanded to twenty-two families and has organized into two church districts. Of similar size is the Old Order community at Marshfield which consists of sixteen families.[6]

The smallest Old Order Amish communities of Fortuna, Douglas County (Dogwood), and Mountain View were of similar size. The Fortuna community began in 1968 and at one point included eighteen families. However, the seven remaining Amish families in the group had moved from the area by fall 1974. The Mountain View settlement was originated in 1966 with seven of the first families moving from Ohio, one from Michigan, and one from Indiana. Several of the original

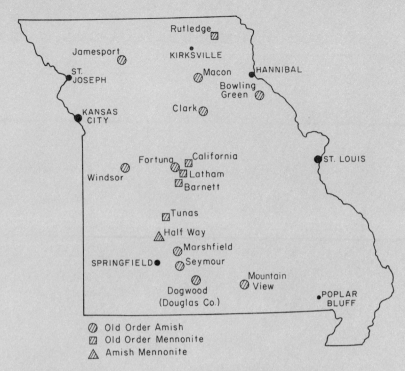

MAP 4. Old Order Amish and Mennonite settlements in Missouri.

families have moved away leaving five in the area. The Douglas County (Dogwood) settlement is also quite recent and includes a small membership.[7] A new Missouri community containing less than a dozen families was initiated in the spring of 1974 at Windsor.

An additional Amish community near Half Way, Missouri, belongs to neither the Old Order or the Beachy but is "Amish Mennonite." Unlike most liberal Amish groups, the Half Way members did not split from the Old Order but formerly belonged to a liberal Mennonite church in Cass County, Missouri. In 1912 a group left that church and moved to Tampico, Illinois. They remained there until the fall of 1964 when around forty families began moving to the Half Way area. Some differences arose among the membership and in 1970 about twenty families left the group and moved to Mena, Arkansas, leaving thirty-two families. Like the Beachy Amish, the Half Way group allow black automobiles and the use of electricity and telephones but not radios, television sets, and the taking of photographs. Clothing styles are also

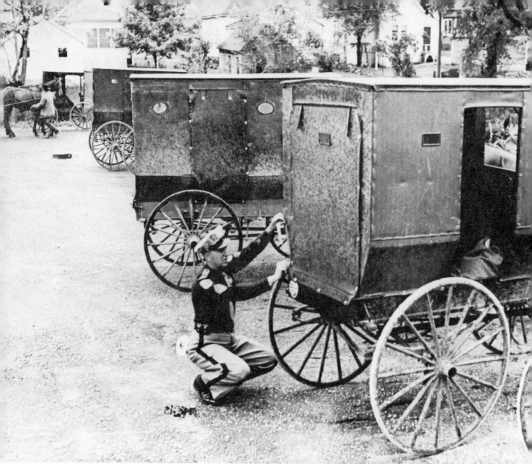

REFLECTOR TAPE APPLIED FOR SAFETY.

similar; both men and women wear plain clothing, while the women cover their heads with a prayer bonnet and the married men wear beards.[8]

The Fortuna Old Order Amish community is of special significance because of its short-lived existence. When it was started in 1968, the earliest families had every indication that the community would increase in size and become a major settlement. The reason for the community's decline is that a large group of conservative Pennsylvania Mennonites (known popularly as the "Black Bumper" Mennonites because they paint the chrome on their cars black) has moved into the area. This group has grown rapidly and includes more than fifty families. The effect of their settlement has been to push up land prices to the point where the Amish feel they are unable to purchase additional land in the area. Since they see no opportunity for their group to expand, and particularly no hope for the next Amish generation in terms of land purchases, they have decided to move to other communities. Several families moved back to their previous homes in Bronson, Michigan, two families purchased farms in the Bloomfield, Iowa, area, and one family relocated in Illinois.[9]

The experience of the Fortuna group points up another aspect of Amish mobility—the survival rate of new communities. The Amish have no way of anticipating if other religious groups will select their chosen area for settlement and, although they can control which members of their own group will join them, they cannot control the settlement of groups such as the conservative Mennonites. When this situation occurs, the Amish have no recourse other than to select a new area for settlement or move to other previously established communities. Although few Amish communities experience the need to disband so quickly, this experience foreshadows problems that the Amish could well face in the years to come. The Old Order Amish are only part of the large contingent that carry the label, Plain People, and many of these groups may (like the Black Bumper Mennonites) look increasingly to the Midwest for their future land needs. As these groups, along with the Beachy Amish and the Old Order Amish, grow in number and continue their expansion policies, there will be more and more competition for moderately priced land in states such as Missouri, Minnesota, and Iowa. Land prices will inevitably rise and availability of land will of necessity decline. As these conditions develop, land needs will become an even greater problem facing future generations of Old Order Amish.

MISSOURI CONSERVATIVE MENNONITE SETTLEMENTS

Because of similarities between the more conservative Mennonites and the Beachy and Old Order Amish in the areas of dress, occupation, means of travel, and religious beliefs, confusion frequently arises regarding which group has settled where and their appropriate religious identification. Because of this widespread confusion it seems appropriate to include a brief discussion of the larger conservative Mennonite groups that have settled in Missouri.

One of the most conservative of these groups, other than the Amish, is the Old Order Mennonites. This group separated from the Mennonite Church between 1871 and 1900 because they wanted to maintain the "old order" of religious worship. During that time span, four Old Order Mennonite divisions came into being in Indiana and Ohio; Ontario; Lancaster County, Pennsylvania; and Rockingham County, Virginia. These four groups all recognized common religious convictions and commitments. They did not approve of holding Sunday school or evangelistic meetings and opposed any change in church ritual or decorum. They continued to use the German language as frequently as possible in their church services.[10] Sometimes the name "Wisler Mennonites" is used instead of Old Order Mennonites because Jacob Wisler, an ordained Mennonite minister, was a key figure in the first dispute that eventually led to the formation of the group. There is also, within each of the four major divisions, the practice of using the bishops' names to denote their group. In Lancaster County, for example, the Old Order Mennonites were originally called the "Martinites" because Jonas Martin played the major role in the development of that schism. Since 1924 this group has called them- selves "Horning people" because during the 1920s their bishop was Moses Horning.[11]

The first Old Order Mennonites to settle in Missouri were known as the "Stauffer Mennonites." The original group moved to Tunas, Missouri, in 1962 from St. Mary's County, Maryland, along with members from Pennsylvania; fourteen families comprise the group. The Stauffer group originated earlier than the main body of Old Order Mennonites when they split off from the Lancaster Mennonite Con- ference in 1845. Certain members of that conference could not agree on treatment of an orphan child adopted by one of the members. Those that objected to the bishop's decision in the matter formed a new group led by Jacob Stauffer and Jacob Weber. Since 1845 this one group has divided into six, with one faction eventually locating at Loveville in St. Mary's County, Maryland. In total these six groups number about 300 members and are affiliated with the Old Order Mennonite Church. The members do not own automobiles or use tractors for their farming. They dress plainly, similar to the Old Order Amish. They maintain separate church meeting houses but do not hold Sunday school.[12]

The second group of Old Order Mennonites to locate in Missouri came primarily from Lancaster County, Pennsylvania. They settled near Barnett, Missouri, in October 1970 and have grown very rapidly, numbering fifty families with a total population of 325 people. They do not use automobiles, but like the Old Order Amish they use horses and buggies for transportation and are sometimes referred to as "the horse and buggy Mennonites."[13]

In November 1970 the most recent group of Old Order Mennonites, more specifically known as the Horning Mennonites of the Weaverland Conference, started a new settlement in Missouri. The first families settled near Latham and California, but the main group selected land in northeastern Missouri. The first families purchased land in Scotland County in 1973, and within one year the group grew to approximately forty-five families, including Mennonites from Lancaster, Berks, Lebanon, and York counties in Pennsylvania. The group decided to leave the East because of soaring land prices (some farmland was selling for as high as $3,500 per acre) and dense population. The Old Order Mennonites selected northeast Missouri because not only was land moderately priced but many farms were then for sale or would be in the near future. Settlement in that region assured the Mennonites that additional land would be available for future expansion. Community members believe that more Pennsylvania brethren will also be moving to northeast Missouri, since those who live there are highly pleased with their new community.[14]

AMISH SETTLEMENTS IN MINNESOTA

The first Old Order Amish community to be established in Minnesota is located near Wadena. The settlement was started by two families from Medford, Wisconsin, in January 1973, and they were joined later by others from Medford and Cashton, Wisconsin, as well as families from Milton, Iowa, and Anabel, Missouri.[15] The community numbers about ten families.

A Beachy Amish community also is located around Grove City. In 1957 two families from the Hutchinson, Kansas, area initiated the settlement. Thirteen families make up the group.[16]

A second Old Order Amish community has been started near Canton. Beginning in March 1974, families from the Mount Eaton, Ohio, area began to move into the region. The original four families decided to look for land in another part of the country because in their region it was becoming not only scarce but very costly. They looked in Michigan, Wisconsin, and other parts of Minnesota before they decided on the Canton area. They selected the present site because the land appeared to be good and the acreages contained timbered areas. Since the Amish heat their homes with wood-burning stoves, the latter consideration was important. The present families are optimistic about their selection and predict that within the next few years considerably more families—perhaps as many as fifty to one hundred—will relocate in Minnesota.[17]

MAP 5. Old Order and Beachy Amish settlements in Minnesota.

THE FUTURE OF THE OLD ORDER AMISH

The Old Order Amish along with other groups of the Plain People have rediscovered the trans-Mississippi West. It appears that during the remainder of the 1970s and the 1980s the movement of Old Order Amish into Minnesota, Iowa, and Missouri will remain steady or perhaps even increase. Another state that could possibly become the site of Amish settlement is Arkansas, where there is a small Beachy Amish congregation at Mountain View and an Amish Mennonite group at Mena.

The Amish succeeded initially in North America because they were able to satisfy certain basic needs. Not faced with religious discrimination or legal barriers, they were free to purchase land, make primary settlements, achieve at least semiisolation, and have complete freedom in their religious thinking and practices. The same conditions prevailed as later generations of Amish left Pennsylvania and migrated to other regions of the United States. Within that framework of New World success, mobility has played an exceedingly important role. When faced with high land prices and scarcity of land, movements to new areas were possible without loss of prestige among the Amish population as a whole. Not only did relocation satisfy economic needs but, perhaps even more important, it provided an outlet for dissident members. If an Old Order Amish family believed their bishop was too harsh in his judgments, whether that community was in Pennsylvania or Ohio or Missouri, they had total freedom to relocate in another Old Order community; or if they could persuade several other families to join them, they could seek an area for starting a new Amish settlement. In the latter case they would have considerably more freedom to shape the rules of conduct and would no doubt be more satisfied with the community. Thus their societal attitude toward mobility provides a safety valve for all types of economic problems or personal discontent.

However, this range of land choices could become considerably more limited. Competition for agricultural land is increasing and prices are rising steadily. The Old Order Amish, given their particular type of agricultural operations and outmoded equipment, do well in the prairie states where they can practice intensive agriculture on small acreages. Movement westward into the Great Plains region would place them in an area where extensive farming is a necessity. Successful farming in the Great Plains requires large acreages and the use of modern equipment, both of which are rejected by the Amish. The Hutterite colonies in South Dakota, also of Anabaptist heritage, have succeeded because of their ability to innovate in agricultural methods and utilize modern farm machinery and technology. Movement into the Great Plains area would require a total reorganization and readjustment for the Old Order Amish, and it is highly unlikely that such a change would take place. Therefore, there will be a natural western barrier for these people as they continue their search for new settlement areas in the years to come. If and when settlement is no longer feasible in areas like Missouri, Iowa, Minnesota, and Arkansas, the Amish will be faced with making major changes in their life-style or movement to new frontiers outside the United States.

Migration to other countries, however, raises another consideration. As more and more Old Order Amish groups move outside the United States, the more difficult it will become to maintain close contact among communities. There is much interaction between Old Order groups in the United States, and this undoubtedly contributes to the unity and brotherhood experienced by all members. If dispersement continues, separatist tendencies might well develop among the different populations, leading to permanent schisms.

Again of special significance is the mobility feature. The Old Order Amish are today deeply entrenched in areas like southeastern Pennsylvania and northeastern Ohio, and no matter how many new communities are started in the trans-Mississippi West, these older communities will remain strong. The older they are, however, the more ossified they become and the more necessary it is to have additional areas for the formation of new communities. As land becomes increasingly unavailable and expansion limited, many Amish can continue to exist in their settled areas but without the feature of the safety valve. The dissidents will then remain within the older communities and undoubtedly agitate for change or leave the group completely. Either way, Amish society will be altered considerably.

CONCLUSION

Any study or assessment of the ''peculiar people'' known as the Old Order Amish brings into focus several inevitable conclusions. For all their isolation and unchanging ways, they are a competent, flexible people who are most capable of handling their own problems. In areas where disputes have arisen, such as education, and others in which they have requested special consideration, it is interesting to note that they have seldom failed to gain their desired end. Every year more and more Old Order Amish children are attending private Amish schools. It is very doubtful if any more major school court battles will surface in the foreseeable future because the problems are being solved locally or within the framework of state government. Even in less important areas the Amish are finding local and state governments responsive to their needs, as evidenced by the decision of the Iowa State Highway Commission to widen the shoulders of highways around Kalona. Yet another consideration is expansion. More and more families will be moving into existing Amish communities in Minnesota, Iowa, and Missouri; it is also likely that more communities will be initiated in these same areas. But perhaps the most important conclusion of all is that the Old Order Amish are expanding rapidly. For generations, scholars and lay people alike have been predicting that a people who lived in such an isolated state and in such a restricted manner simply could not survive in a rapidly changing world. The Old Order Amish are not only surviving but expanding, and there is every indication they will continue to do so.

Courtesy of the **Des Moines Register and Tribune**

THE VISITOR.

An Act Relating to Compulsory School Attendance and Educational Standards

Senate File 785

BE IT ENACTED BY THE GENERAL ASSEMBLY OF THE STATE OF IOWA:

Section 1. Chapter two hundred ninety-nine, Code 1966, is hereby amended by adding thereto the following new section.

"When members or representatives of a local congregation of a recognized church or religious denomination established for ten (10) years or more within the state of Iowa prior to July 1, 1967, which professes principles or tenets that differ substantially from the objectives, goals, and philosophy of education embodied in standards set forth in section two hundred fifty-seven point twenty-five (257.25) of the Code, and rules adopted in implementation thereof, file with the state superintendent of public instruction proof of the existence of such conflicting tenets or principles, together with a list of the names, ages, and post office addresses of all persons of compulsory school age desiring to be exempted from the compulsory education law and the educational standards law, whose parents or guardians are members of the congregation or religious denomination, the state superintendent, subject to the approval of the state board of public instruction, may exempt the members of the congregation or religious denomination from compliance with any or all requirements of the compulsory education law and the educational standards law for two (2) school years. When the exemption has once been granted, renewal of such exemptions for each succeeding school year may be conditioned by the state superintendent, with the approval of the board, upon proof of achievement in the basic skills of arithmetic, the communicative arts of reading, writing, grammar, and spelling, and an understanding of United States history, history of Iowa, and the principles of American government, by persons of compulsory school age exempted in the preceding year, which shall be determined on the basis of tests or other means of evaluation selected by the state superintendent with the approval of the board. The testing or evaluation, if required, shall be accomplished prior to submission of the request for renewal of the exemption. Renewal requests shall be filed with the state superintendent on or before April 15 of the school year preceding the school year for which the applicants desire exemption.''

ROBERT D. FULTON
President of the Senate

MAURICE E. BARINGER
Speaker of the House

I hereby certify that this bill originated in the Senate and is known as Senate File 785, Sixty-second General Assembly.

AL MEACHAM
Secretary of the Senate

Approved_____, 1967

HAROLD E. HUGHES
Governor

Church Organization Financial Agreement

To _____

_____

Gentlemen:

This is to reliably advise you that_____
of_____,_____, the owner of
a farm located in_____County, Iowa, and located and
described as follows, to-wit:

is a member in good standing of our Church Organization, and as such
member, under the rules of such Church Organization, is entitled to be
re-imbursed for Fire and Windstorm losses upon said farm.

That, in-as-much as you hold a mortgage on this property, any
amount to which he shall become entitled to on account of a fire or
windstorm loss on his farm buildings will be paid by our organization to
you in his stead.

Also, that we will write and notify you if at any time the
said_____shall cease to be entitled to be reimbursed for
such fire or windstorm losses on account of his ceasing to be a member
of such church organization or any other acts or omissions on his part,
or for any other reason.

Such information will be given you in such time that you may
procure insurance on the farm buildings if you so desire.

OLD ORDER AMISH MENNONITE CHURCH
BY _____
Bishop of the_____
_____ District

Kalona, Iowa

The Dortrecht Confession of Faith

Adopted at Dortrecht, Holland, 1632

ARTICLE I

Concerning God and the Creation of all Things

WHEREAS IT IS declared, that "without faith it is impossible to please God" (Heb. 11:6), and that "he that cometh to God must believe that he is, and that he is a rewarder of them that diligently seek him," therefore we confess with the mouth, and believe with the heart, together with all the pious, according to the Holy Scriptures, that there is one eternal, almighty, and incomprehensible God, Father, Son, and Holy Ghost, and none more and none other, before whom no God existed, neither will exist after him. For from him, through him, and in him are all things. To him be blessing, praise, and honor, for ever and ever. Gen. 17:1; Deut. 6:4; Isaiah 46:9; I John 5:7.

In this one God, who "worketh all in all," we believe. Him we confess as the Creator of all things, visible and invisible; who in six days created and prepared "heaven and earth, and the sea, and all things that are therein." And we further believe, that this God still governs and preserves the same, together with all his works, through his wisdom, his might, and the "word of his power." Gen. 5:1, 2; Acts 14:15; I Cor. 12:6; Heb. 1:3.

When he had finished his works and, according to his good pleasure, had ordained and prepared each of them, so that they were right and good according to their nature, being and quality, he created the first man, Adam, the father of all of us, gave him a body formed "of the dust of the ground, and breathed into his nostrils the breath of life," so that he "became a living soul," created by God "in his own image and likeness'' in ''righteousness and true holiness'' unto eternal life. He also gave him a place above all other creatures and endowed him with many high and excellent gifts, put him into the garden of Eden, and gave him a commandment and an interdiction. Thereupon he took a rib from the said Adam, made a woman out of it, brought her to him, and gave her to him as a helpmate and housewife. Consequently he has caused, that from this first man, Adam, all men who ''dwell on the face of the earth,'' have been begotten and have descended. Gen. 1:27; 2:7, 15-17, 22; 5:1; Acts 17:26.

ARTICLE II
The Fall of Man

We believe and confess, that, according to the purport of the Holy Scriptures, our first parents, Adam and Eve, did not long remain in the happy state in which they were created; but did, after being seduced by the deceit and ''subtility'' of the serpent, and envy of the devil, violate the high command of God, and became disobedient to their Creator; through which disobedience ''sin entered into the world, and death by sin;'' so that ''death passed upon all men, for that all have sinned,'' and thereby incurred the wrath of God and condemnation. For which reason our first parents were, by God, driven out of Paradise, to cultivate the earth, to maintain themselves thereon in sorrow, and to ''eat their bread in the sweat of their face,'' until they ''returned to the ground, from which they were taken.'' And that they did, therefore, through this one sin, so far apostatize, depart, and estrange themselves from God, that they could neither help themselves, nor be helped by any of their descendants, nor by angels, nor by any other creature in heaven or on earth, nor be redeemed, or reconciled to God; but would have had to be lost forever, had not God, who pities his creatures, in mercy, interposed in their behalf and made provision for their restoration. Gen. 3:6, 23; Rom. 5:12-19; Psalm 47:8, 9; Rev. 5:3; John 3:16.

ARTICLE III
The Restoration of Man through the Promise of the Coming of Christ

Regarding the restoration of our first parents and their descendants, we believe and confess: That God, notwithstanding their fall, transgression and sin, and although they had no power to help themselves, he was nevertheless not willing that they should be cast off entirely, or be eternally lost; but again called them unto him, comforted them, and showed them that there were yet means with him for their reconciliation; namely, the immaculate Lamb, the Son of God; who "was fore-ordained" to this purpose "before the foundation of the world," and who was promised to them and all their descendants, while they (our first parents) were yet in paradise, for their comfort, redemption, and salvation; yea, who was given to them thenceforward, through faith, as their own; after which all the pious patriarchs, to whom this promise was often renewed, longed and searched, beholding it through faith at a distance, and expecting its fulfillment — expecting that he (the Son of God), would, at his coming, again redeem and deliver the fallen race of man from their sins, their guilt, and unrighteousness. John 1:29; 11:27; I Pet. 1:18, 19; Gen. 3:15; I Jno. 2:1, 2; 3:8; Gal. 4:4, 5.

ARTICLE IV
The Advent of Christ into This World, and the Reason of His Coming

We believe and confess further: That "when the fullness of the time was come," after which all the pious patriarchs so ardently longed, and which they so anxiously awaited — the previously promised Messiah, Redeemer, and Savior, proceeded from God, being sent by Him, and according to the prediction of the prophets and the testimony of the evangelists, came into the world, yea, into the flesh —, so that the word itself thus became flesh and man; and that he was conceived by the Virgin Mary (who was espoused to a man named Joseph, of the house of David), and that she bare him as her first-born son at Bethlehem, "wrapped him in swaddling clothes, and laid him in a manger." John 4:25; 16:28; I Tim. 3:16; Matt, 1:21; John 1:14; Luke 2:7.

Further we believe and confess, that this is the same One, "whose goings forth have been from of old, from everlasting;" who has "neither beginning of days, nor end of life." Of whom it is testified, that he is "Alpha and Omega, the beginning and the end, the first and the last." That this is also he — and none other — who was chosen, promised, and sent; who came into the world; and who is God's only, first, and proper Son; who was before John the Baptist, before Abraham, before the world; yea, who was David's Lord, and who was God of the "whole earth," "the first-born of every creature," who was sent into the world, and himself delivered up the body prepared for him, as "an offering and a sacrifice to God for a sweet smelling savor;" yea, for the comfort, redemption, and salvation for all—of the human race. Micah 5:2; Heb. 7:3; Rev. 1:8; John 3:16; Rom. 8:32; Col. 1:15; Heb. 10:5.

But how, or in what manner, this worthy body was prepared, or how the word became flesh, and he himself man, we content ourselves with the declaration which the worthy evangelists have given and left in their description thereof; according to which we confess with all the saints, that he is the Son of the living God, in whom exist all our hope, comfort, redemption, and salvation, and which we are to seek in no one else. Luke 1:31-35; John 20:31.

Further, we believe and confess by authority of scripture, that when he had ended his course, and "finished" the work for which he was sent into the world, he was, by the providence of God, delivered into the hands of the unrighteous; suffered under the judge, Pontius Pilate, was crucified, died, was buried, rose again from the dead on the third day, and ascended into heaven, where he now sits at the right hand of the Majesty of God on high; from whence he will come again to judge the living and dead. Luke 23:1, 52, 53; 24:5, 6, 51.

Thus we believe the Son of God died—"tasted death for every man," shed his precious blood, and thereby bruised the head of the serpent, destroyed the works of the devil, "blotted out the hand-writing," and purchased redemption for the whole human race; and thus he became the source of eternal salvation to all who from the time of Adam to the end of the world, shall have believed in him, and obeyed him. Gen. 3:15; I John 3:8; Col. 2:14; Rom. 5:18.

ARTICLE V
The Law of Christ, which is the Holy Gospel,
or the New Testament

We also believe and confess, that Christ, before his ascension, established and instituted his New Testament and left it to his followers, to be and remain an everlasting testament, which he confirmed and sealed with his own precious blood; and in which he has so highly commended to them, that neither men or angels may change it, neither take therefrom nor add thereto. Jer. 31:31; Heb. 9:15-17; Matt. 26:28; Gal. 1:8; I Tim. 6:3-5; Rev. 22:18, 19; Matt. 5:18; Luke 21:33.

And that he has caused this Testament (in which the whole counsel and will of his heavenly Father, so far as these are necessary to the salvation of man, are comprehended), to be proclaimed, in his name, through his beloved apostles, messengers, and servants (whom he chose and sent into all the world for this purpose)—to all nations, people and tongues; these apostles preaching repentance and remission of sins; and that he, in said Testament, caused it to be declared, that all men without distinction, if they are obedient, through faith, follow, fulfill and live according to the precepts of the same, are his children and rightful heirs; having thus excluded none from the precious inheritance of eternal salvation, except the unbelieving and disobedient, the headstrong and unconverted; who despise such salvation; and thus by their own actions incur guilt by refusing the same, and "judge themselves unworthy of everlasting life." Mark 16:15; Luke 24:46, 47; Rom. 8:17; Acts 13:46.

ARTICLE VI
Repentance and Amendment of Life

We believe and confess, that, as the "imagination of man's heart is evil from his youth," and consequently inclined to all unrighteousness, sin and wickedness, that therefore, the first doctrine of the precious New Testament of the Son of God is, Repentance and amendment of life. Gen. 8:21; Mark 1:15.

Therefore those who have ears to hear, and hearts to understand, must "bring forth fruits meet for repentance," amend their lives, believe the gospel, "depart from evil and do good," desist from wrong and cease from sinning, "put off the old man with his deeds and put on the new man," which after God is created in "righteousness and true holiness." For neither Baptism, Sacrament, nor church-fellowship, nor any other external ceremony, can, without faith, the new birth, and a change or renewal of life, help, or qualify us, that we may please God, or receive any consolation or promise of salvation from him. Luke 3:8; Eph. 4:22-24; Col. 3:9, 10.

But on the contrary, we must go to God "with a sincere heart in full assurance of faith," and believe in Jesus Christ, as the scriptures speak and testify of him. Through which faith we obtain the pardon of our sins, become sanctified, justified, and children of God; yea, partakers of his mind, nature and image, as we are born again of God through his incorruptible seed from above. Heb. 10:21, 22; John 7:38; II Pet. 1:4.

ARTICLE VII
Holy Baptism

Regarding baptism, we confess that all penitent believers, who through faith, the new birth and renewal of the Holy Ghost, have become united with God, and whose names are recorded in heaven, must, on such scriptural confession of their faith, and renewal of life, according to the command and doctrine of Christ, and the example and custom of the apostles, be baptized with water in the ever adorable name of the Father, and of the Son, and of the Holy Ghost, to the burying of their sins, and thus to become incorporated into the communion of the saints; whereupon they must learn to observe all things whatever the Son of God taught, left on record, and commanded his followers to do. Matt. 3:15; 28:19, 20; Mark 16:15, 16; Acts 2:38; 3:12, 38; 9:18; 10:47; 16:33; Rom. 6:3, 4; Col. 2:12.

ARTICLE VIII
The Church of Christ

We believe in and confess a visible Church of God, consisting of those, who, as before remarked, have truly repented, and rightly believed; who are rightly baptized, united with God in heaven, and incorporated into the communion of the saints on earth. I Cor. 12:13.

And these, we confess, are a "chosen generation, a royal priesthood, an holy nation," who have the testimony that they are the "bride" of Christ; yea, that they are children and heirs of eternal life — a "habitation of God through the Spirit," built on the foundation of the apostles and prophets, of which "Christ himself is the chief cornerstone" — the foundation on which his church is built. John 3:29; Matt. 16:18; Eph. 2:19-21; Tit. 3:7; I Pet. 1:18, 19; 2:9.

This church of the living God, which he has purchased and redeemed through his own precious blood, and with which he will be — according to his own promise — for her comfort and protection, "always, even unto the end of the world;" yea, will dwell and walk with her, and preserve her, that no "winds" nor "floods," yea, not even the "gates of hell shall prevail against her" — may be known by her evangelical faith, doctrine, love, and godly conversation; also by her pure walk and practice, and her observance of the true ordinances of Christ, which he has strictly enjoined on his followers. Matt. 7:25; 16:18; 28:20; II Cor. 6:16.

ARTICLE IX
The Office of Teachers and Ministers—Male and
Female—in the Church

Regarding the offices, and election of persons to the same, in the church, we believe and confess: That, as the church cannot exist and prosper, nor continue in its structure, without offices and regulations, that therefore the Lord Jesus has himself (as a father in his house), appointed and prescribed his offices and ordinances, and has given commandments concerning the same, as to how each one should walk therein, give heed to his own work and calling, and do it as it becomes him to do. Eph. 4:11, 12.

For he himself, as the faithful and great Shepherd, and Bishop of our souls, was sent into the world, not to wound, to break, or destroy the souls of men, but to heal them; to seek that which is lost, and to pull down the hedges and partition wall, so as to make out of many one; thus collecting out of Jews and heathen, yea, out of all nations, a church in his name; for which (so that no one might go astray or be lost) he laid down his own life, and thus procured for them salvation, made them free and redeemed them to which blessing no one could help them, or be of service in obtaining it. I Pet. 2:25; Matt. 18:11; Eph. 2:13, 14; John 10:9, 11, 15.

And that he, besides this, left his church before his departure, provided with faithful ministers, apostles, evangelists, pastors, and teachers, whom he had chosen by prayer and supplication through the Holy Spirit, so that they might govern the church, feed his flock, watch over, maintain, and care for the same: yea, do all things as he left them an example, taught them, and commanded them to do; and likewise to teach the church to observe all things whatsoever he commanded them. Eph. 4:11, 12; Luke 6:12, 13; 10:1; Matt. 28:20.

Also that the apostles were afterwards, as faithful followers of Christ and leaders of the church, diligent in these matters, namely, in choosing through prayer and supplication to God, brethren who were to provide all the churches in the cities and circuits, with bishops, pastors, and leaders, and to ordain to these offices such men as took "heed unto themselves and unto the doctrine," and also unto the flock; who were sound in the faith, pious in their life and conversation, and who had — as well within the church as "without" — a good reputation and a good report; so that they might be a light and example in all godliness and good works; might worthily administer the Lord's ordinances — baptism and sacrament — and that they (the brethren sent by the apostles) might also, at all places, where such were to be had, appoint faithful men as elders, who were able to teach others, confirm them in the name of the Lord "with the laying on of hands," and who (the elders) were to take care of all things of which the church stood in need; so that they, as faithful servants, might well "occupy" their Lord's money, gain thereby, and thus "save themselves and those who hear them." I Tim. 3:1; 4:14-16; Acts 1:23, 24; Tit. 1:5; Luke 19:13.

That they should also take good care (particularly each one of the charge over which he had the oversight), that all the circuits should be well provided with almoners, who should have the care and oversight of the poor, and who were to receive gifts and alms, and again faithfully to distribute them amongst the poor saints who were in need, and this in all honesty, as is becoming. Acts 6:3-6.

Also that honorable old widows should be chosen as servants, who, besides the almoners, are to visit, comfort, and take care of the poor, the weak, afflicted, and the needy, as also to visit, comfort, and take care of widows and orphans; and further to assist in taking care of any matters in the church that properly come within their sphere, according to their best ability. I Tim. 5:9, 10; Rom. 16:1, 2.

And as it further regards the almoners, that they (particularly if they are fit persons, and chosen and ordained thereto by the church), may also in aid and relief of the bishops, exhort the church (being, as already remarked, chosen thereto), and thus assist in word and doctrine; so that each one may serve the other from love, with the gift which he has received from the Lord; so that through the common service and assistance of each member, according to his ability, the body of Christ may be edified, and the Lord's vineyard and church be preserved in its growth and structure. II Tim. 2:2.

ARTICLE X
The Lord's Supper

We also believe in and observe the breaking of bread, or the Lord's Supper, as the Lord Jesus instituted the same (with bread and wine) before his sufferings, and also observed and ate it with the apostles, and also commanded it to be observed to his remembrance, as also the apostles subsequently taught and observed the same in the church, and commanded it to be observed by believers in commemoration of the death and sufferings of the Lord—the breaking of his worthy body and the shedding of his precious blood—for the whole human race. So is the observance of this sacrament also to remind us of the benefit of the said death and sufferings of Christ, namely, the redemption and eternal salvation which he purchased thereby, and the great love thus shown to sinful man; whereby we are earnestly exhorted also to love one another—to love our neighbor—to forgive and absolve him—even as Christ has done unto us—and also to endeavor to maintain and keep alive the union and communion which we have with God, and amongst one another; which is thus shown and represented to us by the aforesaid breaking of bread. Matt. 26:26; Mark 14:22; Luke 22:19, 20; Acts 2:42, 46; I Cor. 10:16; 11:23-26.

ARTICLE XI
The Washing of the Saints' Feet

We also confess a washing of the feet of the saints, as the Lord Jesus did not only institute and command the same, but did also himself wash the feet of the apostles, although he was their Lord and master; thereby giving an example that they also should wash one another's feet, and thus do to one another as he did to them; which they also afterwards taught believers to observe, and all this as a sign of true humiliation; but yet more particularly as a sign to remind us of the true washing—the washing and purification of the soul in the blood of Christ. John 13:4-17; I Tim. 5:9, 10.

ARTICLE XII
Matrimony

We also confess that there is in the church of God an ''honorable'' state of matrimony between two believers of the different sexes, as God first instituted the same in paradise between Adam and Eve, and as the Lord Jesus reformed it by removing all abuses which had crept into it, and restoring it to its first order. Gen. 1:27; 2:18, 21-24.

In this manner the apostle Paul also taught and permitted matrimony in the church, leaving it to each one's own choice to enter into matrimony with any person who would unite with him in such state, provided that it was done ''in the Lord,'' according to the primitive order; the words ''in the Lord,'' to be understood, according to our opinion, that just as the patriarchs had to marry amongst their own kindred or generation, so there is also no other liberty allowed to believers under the New Testament Dispensation, than to marry amongst the ''chosen generation,'' or the spiritual kindred of Christ; that is, to such—and none others—as are already, previous to their marriage, united to the church in heart and soul, have received the same baptism, belong to the same church, are of the same faith and doctrine, and lead the same course of life, with themselves. I Cor. 7:39; 9:5; Gen. 24:4; 28:6, 7; Num. 36:6-9.

ARTICLE XIII
The Office of Civil Government

We also believe and confess, that God has instituted civil government, for the punishment of the wicked and the protection of the pious;

and also further, for the purpose of governing the world, countries and cities; and also to preserve its subjects in good order and under good regulations. Wherefore we are not permitted to despise, revile, or resist the same, but are to acknowledge it as a minister of God and be subject and obedient to it, in all things that do not militate against the law, will, and commandments of God; yea, "to be ready to every good work;" also faithfully to pay it custom, tax, and tribute; thus giving it what is its due; as Jesus Christ taught, did himself, and commanded his followers to do. That we are also to pray to the Lord earnestly for the government and its welfare, and in behalf of our country, so that we may live under its protection, maintain ourselves, and "lead a quiet and peaceable life in all godliness and honesty." And further, that the Lord would recompense them (our rulers), here and in eternity, for all the benefits, liberties, and favors which we enjoy under their laudable administration. Rom. 13:1-7; Titus 3:1, 2; I Pet. 2:17; Matt. 17:27; 22:20, 21; I Tim. 2:1, 2.

ARTICLE XIV

Defense by Force

Regarding revenge, whereby we resist our enemies with the sword, we believe and confess that the Lord Jesus has forbidden his disciples and followers all revenge and resistance, and has thereby commanded them not to "return evil for evil, nor railing for railing;" but to "put up the sword into the sheath," or, as the prophets foretold, "beat them into ploughshares." Matt. 5:39, 44; Rom. 12:14; I Pet. 3:9; Isaiah 2:4; Micah 4:3.

From this we see, that, according to the example, life, and doctrine of Christ, we are not to do wrong, or cause offense or vexation to anyone; but to seek the welfare and salvation of all men; also, if necessity should require it, to flee, for the Lord's sake, from one city or country to another, and suffer the "spoiling of our goods," rather than give occasion of offense to anyone; and if we are struck on our "right cheek, rather to turn the other also," than revenge ourselves, or return the blow. Matt. 5:39; 10:23; Rom. 12:19.

And that we are, besides this, also to pray for our enemies, comfort and feed them, when they are hungry or thirsty, and thus by well-doing convince them and overcome the evil with good. Rom. 12:20, 21.

Finally, that we are to do good in all respects, "commending ourselves to every man's conscience in the sight of God," and according to the law of Christ, do nothing to others that we would not wish them to do unto us. II Cor. 4:2; Matt. 7:12; Luke 6:31.

ARTICLE XV
The Swearing of Oaths

Regarding the swearing of oaths, we believe and confess, that the Lord Jesus has dissuaded his followers from and forbidden them the same; that is, that he commanded them to "swear not at all;" but that their "Yea" should be "yea," and their "Nay, nay." From which we understand that all oaths, high and low, are forbidden; and that instead of them we are to confirm all our promises and covenants, declarations and testimonies of all matters, merely with "Yea that is yea," and "Nay that is nay;" and that we are to perform and fulfill at all times, and in all things, to every one, every promise and obligation to which we thus affirm, as faithfully as if we had confirmed it by the most solemn oath. And if we thus do, we have the confidence that no one — not even government itself — will have just cause to require more of us. Matt. 5:34-37; James 5:12; II Cor. 1:17.

ARTICLE XVI
Excommunication or Expulsion from the Church

We also believe in and acknowledge the ban, or excommunication, a separation or spiritual punishment by the church, for the amendment, and not for the destruction, of offenders; so that what is pure may be separated from that which is impure. That is, if a person, after having been enlightened, and received the knowledge of the truth, and has been received into the communion of the saints, does willfully, or out of presumption, sin against God, or commit some other "sin unto death," thereby falling into such unfruitful works of darkness, that he becomes separated from God, and is debarred from his kingdom — that such an one — when his works are become manifest, and sufficiently known to the church — cannot remain in the "congregation of the righteous;" but must, as an offensive member and open sinner, be excluded from the church, "rebuked before all," and "purged out as a leaven," and thus remain until his amendment, as an example and warning to others, and also that the church may be kept pure from such "spots" and "blemishes;" so that not for the want of this, the name of the Lord be blasphemed, the church dishonored, and a stumbling-block thrown in the way of those "without," and finally, that the offender may not be condemned with the world, but that he may again be convinced of the error of his ways, and brought to repentance and amendment of life. Isaiah 59:2; I Cor. 5:5, 6, 12; I Tim. 5:20; II Cor. 13:10.

Regarding the brotherly admonition, as also the instruction of the erring, we are to "give all diligence" to watch over them, and exhort them in all meekness to the amendment of their ways (James 5:19, 20); and in case any should remain obstinate and unconverted, to reprove them as the case may require. In short, the church must "put away from among herself him that is wicked," whether it be in doctrine or life.

ARTICLE XVII
The Shunning of Those Who are Expelled

As regards the withdrawing from, or the shunning of, those who are expelled, we believe and confess, that if any one, whether it be through a wicked life or perverse doctrine — is so far fallen as to be separated from God, and consequently rebuked by, and expelled from, the church, he must also, according to the doctrine of Christ and his apostles, be shunned and avoided by all the members of the church (particularly by those to whom his misdeeds are known), whether it be in eating or drinking, or other such like social matters. In short, that we are to have nothing to do with him; so that we may not become defiled by intercourse with him, and partakers of his sins; but that he may be made ashamed, be affected in his mind, convinced in his conscience, and thereby induced to amend his ways. I Cor. 5:9-11; Rom. 16:17; II Thess. 3:14; Tit. 3:10, 11.

That nevertheless, as well in shunning as in reproving such offender, such moderation and Christian discretion be used, that such shunning and reproof may not be conducive to his ruin, but be serviceable to his amendment. For should he be in need, hungry, thirsty, naked, sick or visited by some other affliction, we are in duty bound, according to the doctrine and practice of Christ and his apostles, to render him aid and assistance, as necessity may require; otherwise the shunning of him might be rather conducive to his ruin than to his amendment. I Thess. 5:14.

Therefore we must not treat such offenders as enemies, but exhort them as brethren, in order thereby to bring them to a knowledge of their sins and to repentance; so that they may again become reconciled to God and the church, and be received and admitted into the same — thus exercising love towards them, as is becoming. II Thess. 3:15.

ARTICLE XVIII
The Resurrection of the Dead and the Last Judgment

Regarding the resurrection of the dead, we confess with the mouth, and believe with the heart, that according to the scriptures — all

men who shall have died or "fallen asleep," will—through the incomprehensible power of God—at the day of judgment, be "raised up"
and made alive; and that these, together with all those who then remain
alive, and who shall be "changed in a moment, in the twinkling of an
eye, at the last trump," shall "appear before the judgment seat of
Christ," where the good shall be separated from the evil, and where
"every one shall receive the things done in his body, according to that
he hath done, whether it be good or bad;" and that the good or pious
shall then further, as the blessed of their Father, be received by Christ
into eternal life, where they shall receive that joy which "eye hath not
seen, nor ear heard, nor hath entered into the heart of man." Yea,
where they shall reign and triumph with Christ for ever and ever. Matt.
22:30-32; 25:31; Dan. 12:2; Job 19:25, 26; John 5:28, 29; I Cor. 15:51,
52; I Thess. 4:13.

And that, on the contrary, the wicked or impious, shall, as the
accursed of God, be cast into "outer darkness;" yea, into eternal,
hellish torments; "where their worm dieth not, and the fire is not
quenched;" and where—according to Holy Scripture—they can expect
no comfort nor redemption throughout eternity. Isaiah 66:24; Matt.
25:46; Mark 9:46; Rev. 14:10, 11.

May the Lord through his grace make us all fit and worthy, that no
such calamity may befall any of us; but that we may be diligent, and so
take heed to ourselves, that we may be found of him in peace, without
spot, and blameless. Amen.

Now these are, as before mentioned, the chief articles of our
general Christian Faith, which we everywhere teach in our
congregations and families, and according to which we profess to live;
and which, according to our convictions, contain the only true Christian
Faith, which the apostles in their time believed and taught; yea, which
they testified to by their lives and confirmed by their deaths; in which
we will also, according to our weakness, gladly abide, live, and die, that
at last, together with the apostles and all the pious we may obtain the
salvation of our souls through the grace of God.

Thus were the foregoing articles of faith adopted and concluded by
our united churches in the city of Dort, in Holland, on the 21st day of
April, in the year of our Lord 1632, and signed by the following
ministers and teachers.

NOTES

CHAPTER 2

1. Zwingli, Huldrych (Ulrich), *Mennonite Encyclopedia,* 1959, Vol. 4, pp. 1052-54.

2. Ibid.

3. John C. Wenger, *Glimpses of Mennonite History* (Scottdale, Pa.: Mennonite Publishing House, 1940), p. 7.

4. Melvin Gingerich, *The Mennonites in Iowa* (Iowa City: State Historical Society of Iowa, 1939), p. 16.

5. Anabaptist, *Encyclopedia,* 1955, Vol. 1, pp. 113-14.

6. Ibid.; Gingerich, *Mennonites,* p. 18.

7. Gingerich, *Mennonites,* pp. 18-22.

8. Melvin Gingerich, The Mennonites in Iowa, *Palimpsest* 60 (1959): 165-67, 171-75; John Hostetler, *Amish Society,* rev. ed. (Baltimore: Johns Hopkins Press, 1968), pp. 24-26.

9. Hostetler, *Amish Society,* p. 24; Victor Peters, *All Things Common: The Hutterian Way of Life* (Minneapolis: University of Minnesota Press, 1965), p. 11.

10. Gingerich, *Mennonites,* pp. 25-26; Hostetler, *Amish Society,* p. 27.

11. Gingerich, *Mennonites,* pp. 27-29.

12. Ibid., pp. 28-29.

13. Hostetler, *Amish Society,* p. 28.

14. Ibid., pp. 30-31; Amish Division, *Encyclopedia,* Vol. 1, p. 90; Gingerich, *Mennonites,* pp. 30-31.

15. Amish Division, *Encyclopedia,* Vol. 1, p. 90.

16. J. C. Getz, Economic Organization and Practices of the Old Order Amish of Lancaster County, Pennsylvania, *Mennonite Quarterly Review,* 20 (1956):63; Walter Kollmorgen, *Culture of a Contemporary Rural Community,* Rural Life Studies 106 (Washington, D.C.: USGPO, 1942), pp. 19-20; Fred Knopp, The Amish Know How, *Farm Quarterly* 1 (1946):88.

17. Hostetler, *Amish Society,* p. 42; Getz, Economic Organization, p. 64.

18. Kollmorgen, *Culture,* p. 19; Knopp, The Amish, p. 91.

19. Old Order Amish, *Encyclopedia,* Vol. 4, p. 45.

20. Calvin George Bachman, The Old Order Amish of Lancaster County, in *Pennsylvania German Society: Proceedings and Addresses* (Norristown:

Norristown Herald, 1942), p. 51; Kollmorgen, *Culture,* p. 3; Knopp, The Amish, p. 94.

21. Gingerich, Mennonites, *Palimpsest,* pp. 225-26; Iowa State Department of Agriculture, *Iowa Book of Agriculture* (Des Moines: State of Iowa, 1968), pp. 327-37.

22. Hostetler, *Amish Society,* p. 265.

23. Amish Mennonites, *Encyclopedia,* Vol. 1, p. 97.

24. Ibid.; Conservative Amish Menonite Conference, *Encyclopedia,* Vol. 1, p. 702; Hostetler, *Amish Society,* p. 266.

25. Beachy Amish Churches, *Encyclopedia,* Vol. 1, p. 254.

26. Amish Mennonites, *Encyclopedia,* Vol. 1, p. 97.

27. Gingerich, *Mennonites,* pp. 53-56.

28. Ibid., pp. 93-112.

29. Ibid., pp. 113-23.

30. Ibid., p. 124.

31. Ibid., p. 133.

32. Ibid., pp. 311-12.

33. Ibid., pp. 59-66.

34. Old Order Amish Community, Milton, Iowa, private interviews, November 1972. Because of the desire of the interviewed persons to remain anonymous, specific names have been omitted. This information has been recorded, however, and is on file. General Conference Mennonite Community, Pulaski, Iowa, private interview, November 1972.

35. Gingerich, *Mennonites,* pp. 57-66, 329-33.

36. Ibid., pp. 333-36; Sanford Yoder, The Amish in Wright County, *Palimpsest* (1962):401-32.

37. Gingerich, *Mennonites,* pp. 336-37.

CHAPTER 3

1. Old Order Amish Community, Kalona, Iowa, private interviews, March 1971.

2. John Hostetler, *Amish Society,* rev. ed. (Baltimore: Johns Hopkins Press, 1968), p. 51.

3. Ibid., p. 135; Melvin Gingerich, *Mennonite Attire through Four Centuries* (Breinigsville, Pa.: The Pennsylvania German Society, 1970), pp. 96-108.

4. Hostetler, *Amish Society,* pp. 106-9; Kalona interviews, March 1971 and October 1974.

5. Kalona interview, March 1971.

6. Des Moines *Register,* Apr. 17, 1974, pp. 1, 4.

7. Kalona interviews, March 1971.

8. Ibid.

9. John Umble, Amish Ordination Charges, *Mennonite Quarterly Review* (October 1939):236.

10. Hostetler, *Amish Society,* p. 52.

11. Ibid., p. 120.

12. Ibid.; Kalona interviews, March 1971.

CHAPTER 4

1. John Hostetler, *Amish Society,* rev. ed. (Baltimore: Johns Hopkins Press, 1968), pp. 9-10; Fredric Klees, *The Pennsylvania Dutch* (New York: Macmillan, 1950), p. 48.

2. Old Order Amish Community, Kalona, Iowa, private interviews, April 1970.

3. Ibid.

4. Ibid.

5. Walter Kollmorgen, *Culture of a Contemporary Rural Community,* Rural Life Studies 106 (Washington, D.C.: USGPO, 1942), pp. 22, 50-52.

6. Old Order Amish Community, Kalona and Milton, Iowa, private interviews, September 1972.

7. Kalona interviews, March 1971; Milton interviews, October 1972.

8. Kalona interviews with non-Amish business and community leaders, April 1970.

9. Bob Lyons, Coast-to-Coast dealer, private interview, Oelwein, Iowa, July 1971.

10. Milton interviews, September 1972.

11. John W. Bennett, *Hutterian Brethren* (Stanford: Stanford University Press, 1967), p. 165. Bennett first uses the term "ideal of austerity" in regard to the Hutterites, but it is equally applicable to the Old Order Amish.

12. Kalona non-Amish interviews, April 1970.

13. Kalona interviews, April 1970 and March 1971.

14. Ibid.

15. Ibid.

16. Ibid.

17. Milton interviews, July 1971.

18. Ibid.

19. Ibid.

20. Ibid.

21. Kalona interviews, April 1970.

22. Marie Jackson, private interview, Kalona, Iowa, April 1970.

23. Old Order Amish communities, Kalona interviews March 1971; Buchanan County, interviews July 1973; Milton interviews, November 1972.

24. Sister Rosalie Beck, private interview, Ames, Iowa, June 1971.

CHAPTER 5

1. Old Order Amish Community, Milton, Iowa, private interviews, October 1972.

2. John Hostetler, *Amish Society,* rev. ed. (Baltimore: Johns Hopkins Press, 1968), p. 17.

3. John Hostetler, *Educational Achievement and Life-Styles in a Traditional Society, the Old Order Amish* (Washington, D.C.: U.S. Department of Health, Education and Welfare, 1969), pp. 82-83.

4. Hostetler, *Amish Society,* p. 168.

5. Milton interviews, October 1972.

6. The lowering of the legal age from twenty-one to eighteen does not

appear to have affected the Amish, as they continue to regard twenty-one as the time when their young people reach adulthood.

7. Menno Simons, *The Complete Writings of Menno Simons,* Leonard Verduin, trans., and John C. Wenger, ed. (Scottdale, Pa.: Mennonite Publishing House, 1956), p. 951.

8. James Frier, Washington County Extension Agent, Washington, Iowa, private interview, April 1970.

9. Old Order Amish Community, Kalona, Iowa, private interview, March 1971.

10. Ibid.

11. Carol Franz and Gerhard Franz, Amish School Problem of Hazleton, paper prepared for graduation requirements at Luther College, Decorah, Iowa, January 1969.

12. Old Order Amish communities, Kalona, Buchanan County, and Milton interviews, April 1970, September 1972 and July 1973.

13. Ibid.; John Hostetler and Gertrude Huntington, *Children in Amish Society* (New York: Holt, Rinehart and Winston, 1971), p. 28.

14. Kalona interview, April 1970.

15. Ibid.; Milton interview, September 1972.

16. Verle Heine, chiropractor, Oelwein, Iowa, private interview, August 1970; Kalona, Buchanan County, and Milton interviews, August 1970 and November 1972.

17. Milton interview, November 1972.

18. Ibid.

19. *Budget* (Sugar Creek, Ohio), Jan. 4, 1973, p. 7.

20. Ibid.; Kalona interview, November 1974.

21. Ibid.

22. Kalona interview, July 1971.

23. Hostetler, *Amish Society,* p. 292; Des Moines *Register,* Aug. 14, 1964, p. 5.

24. Hostetler, *Amish Society,* p. 300; Kalona interviews, August 1971.

CHAPTER 6

1. Old Order Amish Community, Buchanan County, Iowa, private interviews, June 1973.

2. Old Order Amish Community, Milton, Iowa, private interviews, November 1972.

3. Mr. and Mrs. Maynard Manske, private interview at Milton, September 1972.

4. Milton interviews, September 1972.

5. Ibid.

6. John Hostetler, *Amish Society,* rev. ed. (Baltimore: Johns Hopkins Press, 1968), p. 330.

7. Milton interviews, September 1972.

8. Ibid.

9. Milton interviews with non-Amish business and community leaders, September, October, and November 1972.

10. Kalona interviews, November 1974.

11. Milton interviews, September, October, and November 1972.

12. Ibid.

13. Milton non-Amish interviews, September, October, and November 1972.

14. Bloomfield *Democrat,* Apr. 1, 1971, p. 7.

15. Bloomfield, Iowa, interviews with non-Amish business and community leaders, September 1972.

16. Hostetler, *Amish Society,* p. 332.

17. Milton interviews, September 1972.

18. Ibid.

19. Milton non-Amish interviews, September, October, and November 1972.

20. The other group is the Hutterites with colonies in South Dakota, North Dakota, Montana, and Canada.

21. Charles Nordhoff, *The Communistic Societies of the United States* (New York: Harper, 1875), pp. 31-43.

22. Martha Browning Smith, The Story of Icaria, *Annals of Iowa* 38 (Summer 1965):233-36.

23. Ibid., pp. 248-51.

24. Ibid., pp. 258-61.

25. Robert S. Fogarty, ed., The Millenial Laws, in *American Utopianism* (Itasca, Ill.: Peacock Publishers, 1972), pp. 14-21.

CHAPTER 7

1. Old Order Amish Community, Buchanan County, Iowa, interview with an Old Order bishop, July 1973. Because of the desire of the interviewed persons to remain anonymous, specific names have been omitted. This information has been recorded, however, and is on file.

2. Ibid.

3. Des Moines *Register,* Sept. 27, 1968, p. 19; Oct. 12, 1968, p. 5; Oct. 18, 1968, p. 3.

4. Levi Miller, ed., *Mennonite Yearbook,* 1973, p. 14.

5. Carol Franz and Gerhard Franz, The Amish School Problem of Hazleton, paper prepared for graduation requirements at Luther College, Decorah, Iowa, January 1969, p. 5; Buchanan County interviews, June 1970.

6. Marie Jackson, private interview, Kalona, Iowa, April 1970.

7. Cedar Rapids *Gazette,* Nov. 14, 1965, p. 1B.

8. Franz, School Problem, p. 11.

9. Donald A. Erickson, The "Plain People" and American Democracy, *Commentary* (January 1968):38.

10. Franz, School Problem, pp. 11, 12.

11. Erickson, "Plain People," p. 38.

12. Ibid., p. 39.

13. Ibid.

14. Ibid., pp. 40, 41.

15. Ibid., p. 42.

16. *Register,* Nov. 11, 1962, pp. 1, 7L.

17. Every interview with Amish and non-Amish people supported this view of Borntrager's position within the community and his role in the school conflict. Kalona Amish also frequently voiced the opinion that the school situation could have been solved peacefully if Borntrager had not unfortunately chosen to make an issue of it.

18. *Register,* Nov. 25, 1962, pp. 1L, 4L.

19. Erickson, "Plain People," p. 42.

20. Franz, School Problem, p. 27.

21. Ibid.

22. *Register,* Nov. 7, 1965, pp. 1L, 6L.

23. *Register,* Nov. 20, 1965, pp. 1, 5.

24. Ibid.

25. *Register,* Nov. 23, 1965, p. 1.

26. *Register,* Nov. 24, 1965, p. 1.

27. Erickson, "Plain People," p. 44.

28. Franz, School Problem, p. 34.

29. *Register,* Feb. 23, 1966, p. 1.

30. *Register,* Mar. 27, 1966, p. 8; *Register,* Feb. 3, 1967, p. 8.

31. *Register,* May 28, 1967, p. 10L.

32. *Register,* July 1, 1967, p. 4. See Appendix A for the complete wording
of this bill.

CHAPTER 8

1. Old Order Amish Community, Kalona, Iowa, private interviews,
August 1971.

2. Bloomfield *Democrat,* Apr. 1, 1971, p. 7.

3. Des Moines *Register,* Apr. 22, 1974, p. 11.

4. See Appendix A for specific wording of Senate File 785, An Act
Relating to Compulsory School Attendance and Education Standards.

5. *Register,* Aug. 13, 1971, p. 13; Aug. 27, 1971, pp. 1, 11.

6. *Register,* May 18, 1973, p. 9.

7. Mrs. Edith Munro, elementary education consultant, private interview
at the State Department of Public Instruction, Des Moines, Iowa, January 1974.

8. Kalona interviews, July 1971; Old Order Amish Community, Milton,
Iowa, private interviews, November 1972.

9. Dale Logan, president, Mid-Prairie School Board, Kalona, Iowa,
private interview, July 1971; also see article entitled, More Amish Get School
exemptions, *Register,* Apr. 22, 1974, p. 11, for reasons advanced by Beachy
Amish in support of their school exemption.

10. Kalona interviews, April 1970 and July 1971.

11. Munro interview.

12. One book that deals with this thesis is *Children Teach Children* by Alan
Gartner, Mary Kohler, and Frank Riessman (New York: Harper & Row, 1971).

13. Munro interview.

14. *Wisconsin* v. *Yoder,* 406 U.S. 224 (1972).

15. *Register,* Nov. 22, 1970, p. 3L.

16. John Hostetler and Gertrude Huntington, *Children in Amish Society*
(New York: Holt, Rinehart and Winston, 1971), p. 79.

17. Ibid., p. 71.

18. Kalona interview, July 1971.

19. Stephen Arons, Compulsory Education: The Plain People Resist,
Saturday Review (Jan. 15, 1972):53.

20. *Wisconsin* v. *Yoder,* 212.

21. Ibid., 224, 232.

22. *Register,* Dec. 14, 1973, p. 1, 6.

23. The three major religious groups in Iowa that provide private education for their offspring are Roman Catholics, Christian Reformed, and Lutherans; *Register,* May 26, 1974, p. 4C.

CHAPTER 9

1. Beachy Amish Churches, *Mennonite Encyclopedia,* 1955, Vol. 1, p. 254.

2. Ibid.

3. Marlan Logan, Beachy Amish in Iowa. Unpublished paper, Iowa State University, 1973, p. 1.

4. *Mennonite Yearbook and Directory* (Scottdale, Pa.: Mennonite Publishing House, 1973), p. 94.

5. Logan, Beachy Amish, pp. 5-6; Beachy Amish Community, Decatur City, Iowa, private interviews, January 1974.

6. Logan, Beachy Amish, p. 5.

7. Ibid., p. 6. Because the Beachy Amish believe in baptism based on confession of faith, the membership number of ninety-nine does not include offspring who have not yet been baptised. The Beachy, like the Old Order, have large families, so the total number of people in this community would be roughly double the baptised members. Typically, there are more unbaptised members in a community than baptised members. John Hostetler, *Amish Society,* rev. ed. (Baltimore: Johns Hopkins Press, 1968), p. 80.

8. Decatur City interviews, January 1974.

9. Logan, Beachy Amish, p. 10.

10. Decatur City interviews, January 1974. Possibly Leon residents were also confused about the present status of the Amanas and did not know that the Amana people dropped the communal basis of economic organization in 1932. Today the Amana Corporation owns the agricultural lands, meat plants, furniture shops, and other operations but each Amana resident owns his or her own home and other private property. An excellent presentation of the Amana story is Barbara Yambura's *A Change and a Parting* (Ames: Iowa State University Press, 1960).

11. Logan, Beachy Amish, p. 12.

12. Decatur City interviews, January 1974.

13. Peace, War and Social Issues, A Statement of the Position of the Amish Mennonite Churches. This statement was officially adopted by the ministerial body of the Beachy Amish constituency at their regular annual meeting at Wellesley, Ontario, Canada, Apr. 18 and 19, 1968, pp. 14, 15.

14. Ibid., pp. 15, 16.

15. Ibid., p. 16.

16. Decatur City interviews, January 1974; Mrs. Edith Munro, elementary education consultant, private interview at state Department of Public Instruction, Des Moines, Iowa, January 1974.

17. Logan, Beachy Amish, p. 17; pamphlet advertising school entitled, Calvary Bible School, Calico Rock, Arkansas, Jan. 1, 1973, Mar. 2, 1973.

18. Logan, Beachy Amish, pp. 2-4.

19. They also quote Romans 12:14; I Peter 3:9; Isaiah 2:4; Micah 4:3. Also see Dortrecht Confession, Article XIV.

20. Peace, War and Social Issues, p. 6.

21. Ibid., p. 8.

22. Decatur City interviews, January 1974.

23. Ibid.

24. Ibid.; Beachy Amish community, Kalona, Iowa, private interviews, March 1971.

25. Logan, Beachy Amish, p. 20.

26. Decatur City interviews, January 1974.

27. Amish Mennonite Aid Overseas Voluntary Service Manual (East Rochester, Ohio: Amish Mennonite Aid, 1967), p. 1.

28. Logan, Beachy Amish, p. 18.

29. Decatur City interviews, January 1974; *Mennonite Yearbook,* p. 94.

30. Decatur City interviews, January 1974.

31. Logan, Beachy Amish, p. 12; Decatur City interviews, January 1974.

CHAPTER 10

1. Old Order Amish members in Kalona estimate that roughly 10 percent of their people leave the Old Order faith. Most do not go very far, however, as many join the Beachy Amish church or another conservative Mennonite congregation.

2. Missouri, *Mennonite Encyclopedia,* 1957, Vol. 3, p. 791; letter from E. J. Miller, member of the Clark, Missouri, Old Order Amish Community and *Budget* correspondent, May 1974.

3. Letter from Mrs. John U. Miller, member of the Jamesport, Missouri, Old Order Amish Community and *Budget* correspondent, March 1974.

4. *Budget,* Jan. 10, 1974, p. 16.

5. E. J. Miller letter; *Budget,* Feb. 14, 1974, p. 9.

6. Letter from Mr. and Mrs. Mahlon Schwartz, members of the Seymour, Missouri, Old Order Amish Community and *Budget* correspondents, April 1974; letter from Sam W. Schrock, member of the Macon, Missouri, Old Order Amish Community and *Budget* correspondent, April 1974; *Budget,* Mar. 14, 1974.

7. Letter from Mr. and Mrs. Menno Borntrager, members of the Fortuna, Missouri, Old Order Amish Community and *Budget* correspondents, March 1974; letter from Melvin L. Yoder, member of the Mountain View, Missouri, Old Order Amish Community and *Budget* correspondent, May 1974; *Budget,* Jan. 31, 1974, p. 1.

8. Letter from Mr. and Mrs. John Blosser, members of the Half Way, Missouri, Amish Mennonite Community and *Budget* correspondents, April 1974.

9. Letter, Borntrager, March 1974.

10. Old Order Mennonites, *Encyclopedia,* 1959, Vol. 4, pp. 47-49.

11. Horning Mennonites, *Encyclopedia,* 1956, Vol. 2, p. 813; letter from Mr. and Mrs. Mark H. Horning, members of the Horning Old Order Mennonite Community (Weaverland Conference), Rutledge, Missouri, and *Budget* correspondents, April 1974.

12. Stauffer Mennonite Church, *Encyclopedia,* Vol. 4, pp. 621-22; letter from Mrs. C. Wenger, member of the Tunas, Missouri, Old Order Mennonite Community and *Budget* correspondent, April 1974. Also, during the 1880s a group of Stauffer Mennonites settled near May City in Osceola County where they maintained a fairly progressive Mennonite community for approximately

thirty years. For a full account see Melvin Gingerich, *The Mennonites in Iowa* (Iowa City: State Historical Society of Iowa, 1939), pp. 337-41.

13. Letter from Miss Ella Rissler, member of the Barnett, Missouri, Old Order Mennonite Community and *Budget* correspondent, May 1974.

14. Letters from Mr. and Mrs. Mark H. Horning and Mr. and Mrs. Ivan High, members of the Horning Old Order Mennonite Community (Weaverland Conference), Rutledge, Missouri, April 1974.

15. *Budget,* Jan. 11, 1973, p. 15; Mar. 15, 1973, p. 15; July 25, 1973, p. 15.

16. Letter from Miss Clara Miller, member of the Grove City, Minnesota, Beachy Amish Community and *Budget* correspondent, March 1974.

17. Des Moines *Register,* May 4, 1974, p. 7.

BIBLIOGRAPHY

A NOTE ON THE SOURCES

A substantial number of scholarly studies have been done on the Old Order Amish. Typically these have centered on communities in Pennsylvania, Indiana, and Ohio, with few works specifically treating life in Iowa. The lack of material on Iowa and the surrounding states is particularly evident since so many new Amish communities have been established in the Midwest since 1950.

The first book written on the Amish was in 1894 by an Iowan, Barthinius L. Wick, and was entitled *The Amish Mennonites*. Of more contemporary interest, however, are the studies conducted since 1939. In that year Melvin Gingerich wrote *The Mennonites in Iowa*, in which he devoted several chapters to the life-style of the Iowa Old Order Amish. In Pennsylvania the pioneer study of the Old Order was done in 1942 by Walter Kollmorgen, *Culture of a Contemporary Rural Community*. Kollmorgen conducted the project as a part of a Rural Life Studies program sponsored by the United States Bureau of Agricultural Economics. *Amish Society,* the first definitive work on the Old Order Amish, was written by John Hostetler in 1963 and revised in 1968. In this sociological study, Hostetler analyzed all facets of Amish life, centering on Amish populations in Pennsylvania and Ohio. Hostetler also has written numerous articles, including an *Annotated Bibliography on the Old Order Amish* published in 1951. Hostetler's most recent work, *Children in Amish Society,* was coauthored with Gertrude Huntington in 1972 and deals primarily with the Amish educational system.

Aside from the Amish material included in Gingerich's book, the only other studies dealing specifically with the Iowa Amish have been in the area of education. The development of the school controversy in

Iowa in the 1960s was covered by Harrell R. Rodgers, Jr., in his opinion and attitude study, *Community Conflict, Public Opinion and the Law*, published in 1969. Donald Hayes treated Old Order Amish education in a general way in his Ph.D. dissertation, "The Iowa Amish and Their Education," completed in 1972.

The following bibliography indicates the sources used in this study as well as including the earliest and most significant Amish studies such as those cited above. It is not intended, however, to be comprehensive regarding all phases of Amish society nor to cover all geographical areas. For those interested in works relating to the Old Order Amish in Pennsylvania, Ohio, and Indiana, the bibliography in Hostetler's *Amish Society* provides a complete listing. For any topic relating to Mennonite history, Mennonite religion, or specific individuals who have been prominent in that church as well as any Mennonite settlement, the four volumes of *The Mennonite Encyclopedia* provide the most complete information.

Books

Bachmann, Calvin George. *The Old Order Amish of Lancaster County, Pennsylvania*. Breinigsville, Pa.: Pennsylvania German Society, 1942. Reprinted in 1961.

Gingerich, Melvin. *The Mennonites in Iowa*. Iowa City: State Historical Society of Iowa, 1939.

————. *Mennonite Attire through Four Centuries*. Breinigsville, Pa.: Pennsylvania German Society, 1970.

Hostetler, John A. *Amish Society*, rev. ed. Baltimore: Johns Hopkins Press, 1968.

————. *An Annotated Bibliography on the Old Order Amish*. Scottdale, Pa.: Mennonite Publishing House, 1951.

Hostetler, John A.; and Huntington, Gertrude. *Children in Amish Society*. New York: Holt, Rinehart and Winston, 1972.

Keim, Albert N. *Compulsory Education and the Amish: The Right Not to Be Modern*. Boston: Beacon Press, 1975.

Kollmorgen, Walter. *Culture of a Contemporary Rural Community: The Old Order Amish of Lancaster County, Pennsylvania*. Rural Life Studies No. 106. Washington, D.C.: USGPO, 1942.

Miller, Levi, ed. *Mennonite Yearbook and Directory*. Sixty-Fourth Yearbook of the Mennonite Church. Scottdale, Pa.: Mennonite Publishing House, 1973.

Mennonite Encyclopedia, 4 vols. Scottdale, Pa.: Mennonite Publishing House; Hillsboro, Kans.: Mennonite Brethren Publishing House;

and North Newton, Kans.: Mennonite Publication Office, 1955-1959.

Rodgers, Harrell R., Jr. *Community Conflict, Public Opinion and the Law.* Columbus, Ohio: Charles E. Merrill, 1969.

Schwieder, Dorothy, ed. Agrarian Stability in Utopian Societies: A Comparison of Economic Practices of Old Order Amish and Hutterites. In *Patterns and Perspectives in Iowa History.* Ames: Iowa State University Press, 1973.

Simons, Menno. *The Complete Writings of Menno Simons,* Leonard Verduin, trans.; John C. Wenger, ed. Scottdale, Pa.: Mennonite Publishing House, 1956.

Warner, J. A.; and Denlinger, J. M. *The Gentle People.* Soudersburg, Pa.: Mill Bridge Museum, 1969.

Wenger, John C. *Glimpses of Mennonite History.* Scottdale, Pa.: Mennonite Publishing House, 1940.

Wick, Barthinius L. *The Amish Mennonites: A Sketch of Their Origin, and of Their Settlement in Iowa.* Iowa City: State Historical Society of Iowa, 1894.

Articles

Arons, Stephen. Compulsory Education: The Plain People Resist. *Saturday Review* (Jan. 15, 1972): 52-57.

Erickson, Donald A. The "Plain People" and American Democracy. *Commentary* (January 1968): 36-44.

————. The Plain People vs. The Common Schools. *Saturday Review* (Nov. 19, 1966): 85-87, 102-3.

Getz, J. C. Economic Organization and Practices of the Old Order Amish of Lancaster County, Pennsylvania. *Mennonite Quarterly Review* 20(1956): 53-60, 98-127.

Gingerich, Melvin. The Mennonites in Iowa. *Palimpsest* 60 (1959): 161-224.

Guengerich, S. D. The History of the Amish Settlement in Johnson County, Iowa. *Mennonite Quarterly Review* 3(1929):243-48.

Knopp, Fred. The Amish Know How. *Farm Quarterly* 1(1946): 86-99, 128-32.

Peace, War and Social Issues, A Statement of the Position of the Amish Mennonite Churches. Beachy Amish annual meeting, Wellesley, Ontario, Canada, 1968.

Wittmer, Joe; and Moser, Arnold. Counseling the Old Order Amish Child. *Elementary School Guidance and Counseling* (May 1974): 263-71.

Amish Publications

Blackboard Bulletin. Aylmer, Ontario, Canada: Pathway Publishing
  Corporation.
Family Life. Aylmer, Ontario, Canada: Pathway Publishing Cor-
  poration.

Newspapers

Bloomfield *Democrat* (Bloomfield, Iowa)
Des Moines *Register* (Des Moines, Iowa)
Budget (Sugar Creek, Ohio)

Unpublished Works

Franz, Gerhard; and Franz, Carol. The Amish School Problem in
  Hazleton. Unpublished paper, Luther College, 1969.
Hayes, Donald Paul. The Iowa Amish and Their Education. Un-
  published Ph.D. dissertation, University of Iowa, 1972.
Logan, Marlan. Beachy Amish in Iowa. Unpublished paper, Iowa State
  University, 1973.
Schwieder, Dorothy. A Study of the Hutterites as a Frontier Utopian
  Movement. Unpublished M.S. thesis, Iowa State University, 1968,

Fictionalized Works

McCleery, Jean M. *Yesterday—Today—Tomorrow.* New York: Carlton
  Press, 1971.
Miller, Clara B. *The Tender Herb.* Scottdale, Pa.: Herold Press, 1968.
———. *The Crying Heart.* Scottdale, Pa.: Herold Press, 1962.
Neidermyer, Dan. *Jonathan.* Scottdale, Pa.: Herold Press, 1973.
Yoder, Joseph W. *Amish Traditions.* Scottdale, Pa.: Herold Press,
  1950.
———. *Rosanna of the Amish.* Scottdale, Pa.: Herold Press, 1940.
———. *Rosanna's Boys.* Scottdale, Pa.: Herold Press, 1947.

Legal Documents

Wisconsin v. *Yoder,* 406 (U.S. Supreme Court, May 15, 1972).

Interviews

Kalona, Iowa
Old Order Amish

Mr. and Mrs. Tobias J. Miller
Mr. and Mrs. Ben L. Yoder

Mr. and Mrs. Eddie Miller
Mr. and Mrs. Henry Bender
Mr. and Mrs. Benedict J. Yoder
Miss Amanda Hochstetler
Miss Eunice Miller
Bishop and Mrs. Truman Miller
Joe C. Ropp
Elija Miller
Bishop and Mrs. Glen L. Bender

Non-Amish Residents

Miss Marie Jackson
Ferd Skola
James Frier
Chester Miller
Glen Guengerich
Marlan Logan
Dale Logan
Miss Julie Hartzler
Thomas A. Miller

Milton, Iowa, and Vicinity
Old Order Amish

Bishop and Mrs. Chris Kauffman
Mr. and Mrs. David Stutzman
Mrs. Daniel Beachy
Mr. and Mrs. Mervin Hershberger
Mr. and Mrs. Mahlon Mullet
Joe Hostetler

Non-Amish Residents

Mr. and Mrs. Maynard Manske
Mr. and Mrs. Homer Parcell
Bill Strait
Red Roberts
Mr. and Mrs. Ralph Arnold (Douds)
William Byers (Ottumwa)
Miss Linda Nixon (Cantril)
Danny Manske
Glee Bullock

Mr. and Mrs. Ed Nixon (Cantril)
Mrs. Doris Harrison
Mr. and Mrs. Verle Arnold (Bloomfield)
Mel Powers (Keosauqua)
Julien Campbell (Bloomfield)
Stan Rogers (Bloomfield)

Buchanan County
Old Order Amish

Mrs. Andy Kurtz
Jonas Helmuth
Bishop and Mrs. Levi Borntreger
Mr. and Mrs. Mervin Hershberger
    (former Buchanan County residents)

Non-Amish Residents

Mrs. Mary Lacock
Mr. and Mrs. Joe Miller
Mr. and Mrs. Bob Lyons
Dr. Verle Heine
Mr. and Mrs. Vargi Vargason
Mr. and Mrs. Roland Seamans
Richard Seamans
The Reverend Robert Engbrecht
Mrs. Eunice Corcoran
Mr. and Mrs. Ron Graf

Leon, Iowa
Beachy Amish Community

Mr. and Mrs. John Yutzy
Enos Mast

INDEX